D1757815

Guidelines for
LAND-USE PLANNING

FAO Development Series **1**

ISSN 1020-0819

Guidelines for

LAND-USE
PLANNING

Prepared by the
Soil Resources, Management and Conservation Service
under the guidance of the
Inter-Departmental Working Group on Land Use Planning

FOOD AND AGRICULTURE ORGANIZATION OF THE UNITED NATIONS
Rome, 1993

David Lubin Memorial Library Cataloguing in Publication Data

FAO, Rome (Italy)
Guidelines for land-use planning.
(FAO Development Series No. 1)
ISBN 92-5-103282-3

1. Land use 2. Planning
I. Title II. Series

FAO code: 59 AGRIS: E11

Foreword

Land resources are limited and finite. If human populations continue to increase at the present rate there will be twice as many people in the world in about 60 years. There is therefore an increasingly urgent need to match land types and land uses in the most rational way possible, so as to maximize sustainable production and satisfy the diverse needs of society while at the same time conserving fragile ecosystems and our genetic heritage.

Land-use planning is fundamental to this process. It is a basic component, whether we are considering mountain ecosystems, savannahs or coastal zones, and underlies the development and conservation of forestry, range and inland as well as coastal resources. Land-use planning is also a key element in all types of agricultural development and conservation.

These guidelines are intended to help all those involved in planning the development, management and conservation of rural land. This includes not only specialists in land-use planning but also ministers of agriculture and environment, extension workers, forest officers, village leaders and many others who contribute to or are involved in planning the use of land resources. This publication provides an overview for people who commission and adopt land-use plans. It also provides practical advice for those who have to prepare such plans.

Land-use planning is sometimes misunderstood as being a process where planners tell people what to do, i.e. a typical top-down situation. In this publication, land-use planning means the systematic assessment of physical, social and economic factors in such a way as to assist and encourage land users to select land-use options that increase their productivity, are sustainable and meet the needs of society. Farmers and other land users can, and should, take an active part in land-use planning, bringing to bear their special knowledge of problems, constraints and needs for improvement.

This is not an instruction manual. It is impractical to provide instructions that are sufficiently comprehensive to apply to the diversity of climate, land resources and economic and social conditions for which land-use plans are needed. However, the principles and methods outlined here provide a framework for the development of detailed procedures that will deal directly with the specific problems and opportunities of land use in individual countries.

Land-use planning is an extremely complex subject, combining physical, social and economic aspects of land use with an assessment of potential future needs. We would, therefore, welcome comments and suggestions as to how these guidelines could be improved. We also invite any person or group who is interested in carrying out case-studies on particular land-use planning programmes or projects to contact us regarding possible collaboration.

C.H. Murray
Chairman, Inter-Departmental Working Group
on Land Use Planning, FAO

PLATE 1
Good land use, closely matched to the potential of the land in a long-settled area

Contents

Boxes

Tables

Figures

Plates

Acknowledgements

Many people have participated in the development of these guidelines, including FAO field staff, members of Sub-Group I of the FAO Inter-Departmental Group on Land Use Planning, under the chairmanship of Maurice Purnell. Their contributions are gratefully acknowledged. The first draft was prepared by Devon Nelson and the second by David Dent. Successive drafts were reviewed at two expert consultations, held in Rome in 1986 and 1989, and comments were received from many people – of particular value were those from the Working Group, chaired by G. Robertson at the 1989 consultation, and those from J. Dixon and Robert Ridgway. Final editing was done by Anthony Young and FAO staff in Rome.

Summary

Guidelines for land-use planning is primarily intended for people engaged in making land-use plans, or those training to do so, including staff of local government, national agencies and international projects in developing countries. The guidelines also provide an overview of land-use planning for administrators and decision-makers.

Chapter 1 describes the nature and purpose of land-use planning: what it is, why it is needed, who benefits from it and who carries it out. It describes the different levels or scales at which planning is carried out and identifies the people involved: the land users, the decision-makers and the planning team.

Chapter 2 outlines the work involved in terms of ten steps, from the first meeting between planners and potential users to the implementation of the land-use plan. These steps provide a logical sequence of activities, each of which has a purpose.

Chapter 3 describes the same steps in more detail. Again, flexibility will be needed in adapting each step to the specific circumstances of a particular plan. For each step, a *Checklist* is given.

Chapter 4 is for reference. It indicates some of the technical methods that are available for planning, with references to sources of detailed information.

Technical terms are defined in the *Glossary*.

HOW TO USE THE GUIDELINES

Planning is a learning process and needs to be flexible. It can best be learned by doing. The ten steps outlined in Chapters 2 and 3 need not be followed rigidly, but can be adapted to circumstances. However, thought should be given to the purpose of each step and to whether it is needed in a particular plan. The guidelines can be adapted to local conditions, either by producing national land-use planning handbooks or simply by listing the needs, tasks and responsibilities for a particular project as well as allowing for adjustments on the job.

Chapter 1
Nature and scope

WHAT IS LAND-USE PLANNING?

There is bound to be conflict over land use. The demands for arable land, grazing, forestry, wildlife, tourism and urban development are greater than the land resources available. In the developing countries, these demands become more pressing every year. The population dependent on the land for food, fuel and employment will double within the next 25 to 50 years. Even where land is still plentiful, many people may have inadequate access to land or to the benefits from its use. In the face of scarcity, the degradation of farmland, forest or water resources may be clear for all to see but individual land users lack the incentive or resources to stop it.

Land-use planning is the systematic assessment of land and water potential, alternatives for land use and economic and social conditions in order to select and adopt the best land-use options. Its purpose is to select and put into practice those land uses that will best meet the needs of the people while safeguarding resources for the future. The driving force in planning is the need for change, the need for improved management or the need for a quite different pattern of land use dictated by changing circumstances.

All kinds of rural land use are involved: agriculture, pastoralism, forestry, wildlife conservation and tourism. Planning also provides guidance in cases of conflict between rural land use and urban or industrial expansion, by indicating which areas of land are most valuable under rural use.

WHEN IS LAND-USE PLANNING USEFUL?

Two conditions must be met if planning is to be useful:

- the need for changes in land use, or action to prevent some unwanted change, must be accepted by the people involved;
- there must be the political will and ability to put the plan into effect.

Where these conditions are not met, and yet problems are pressing, it may be appropriate to mount an awareness campaign or set up demonstration areas with the aim of creating the conditions necessary for effective planning.

MAKING THE BEST USE OF LIMITED RESOURCES

Our basic needs of food, water, fuel, clothing and shelter must be met from the land, which is in limited supply. As population and aspirations increase, so land becomes an increasingly scarce resource.

Land must change to meet new demands yet change brings new conflicts between competing uses of the land and between the interests of individual land users and the common good. Land taken for towns and industry is no longer available for farming; likewise, the development of new farmland competes with forestry, water supplies and wildlife.

Planning to make the best use of land is not a new idea. Over the years, farmers have made plans season after season, deciding what to grow and where to grow it. Their decisions have been made according to their own needs, their knowledge of the land and the technology, labour and capital available. As the size of the area, the number of people involved and the complexity of the problems increase, so does the need for information and rigorous methods of analysis and planning.

However, land-use planning is not just farm planning on a different scale; it has a further dimension, namely the interest of the whole community.

Planning involves anticipation of the need for change as well as reactions to it. Its objectives are set by social or political imperatives and must take account of the existing situation. In many places, the existing situation cannot

PLATE 2
A land-use problem: illegal clearance of forest in Sri Lanka

continue because the land itself is being degraded (Plate 2). Examples of unwise land use include: the clearance of forest on steeplands or on poor soils for which sustainable systems of farming have not been developed; overgrazing of pastures; and industrial, agricultural and urban activities that produce pollution. Degradation of land resources may be attributed to greed, ignorance, uncertainty or lack of an alternative but, essentially, it is a consequence of using land today without investing in tomorrow.

Land-use planning aims to make the best use of limited resources by:
- assessing present and future needs and systematically evaluating the land's ability to supply them;
- identifying and resolving conflicts between competing uses, between the needs of individuals and those of the community, and between the needs of the present generation and those of future generations;
- seeking sustainable options and choosing those that best meet identified needs;
- planning to bring about desired changes;
- learning from experience.

There can be no blueprint for change. The whole process of planning is iterative and continuous. At every stage, as better information is obtained, a plan may have to be changed to take account of it.

GOALS

Goals define what is meant by the "best" use of the land. They should be specified at the outset of a particular planning project. Goals may be grouped under the three headings of efficiency, equity and acceptability and sustainability.

Efficiency. Land use must be economically viable, so one goal of development planning is to make efficient and productive use of the land. For any particular land use, certain areas are better suited than others. Efficiency is achieved by matching different land uses with the areas that will yield the greatest benefits at the least cost.

Efficiency means different things to different people, however. To the individual land user, it means the greatest return on capital and labour invested or the greatest benefit from the area available. Government objectives are more complex: they may include improving the foreign exchange situation by producing for export or for import substitution.

Equity and acceptability. Land use must also be socially acceptable. Goals include food security, employment and security of income in rural areas. Land improvements and redistribution of land may be undertaken to reduce inequality or, alternatively, to attack absolute poverty.

One way of doing this is to set a threshold standard of living to which those of target groups should be raised. Living standards may

---

Box 1
The planning process

Land-use planning can be expressed in the following questions:

- **What is the present situation?**

- **Is change desirable? If so:**
  - **What needs to be changed?**
    Land-use problems and opportunities are identified by discussions with the people involved and by the study of their needs and the resources of the area.
  - **How can the changes be made?**
    Planners seek a range of ways to make use of the opportunities and solve the problems.
  - **Which is the best option?**
    Decision-makers choose the best option, based on forecasts of the results of implementing each alternative.
  - **How far is the plan succeeding?**
    Once a land-use plan is put into effect, planners monitor progress made towards its goals and change the plan if necessary.

include levels of income, nutrition, food security and housing. Planning to achieve these standards then involves the allocation of land for specific uses as well as the allocation of financial and other resources.

Sustainability. Sustainable land use is that which meets the needs of the present while, at the same time, conserving resources for future generations. This requires a combination of production and conservation: the production of the goods needed by people now, combined with the conservation of the natural resources on which that production depends so as to ensure continued production in the future.

A community that destroys its land forfeits its future. Land use has to be planned for the community as a whole because the conservation of soil, water and other land resources is

often beyond the means of individual land users.

Trade-offs between conflicting goals

Clearly, there are conflicts between these goals. More equity may mean less efficiency. In the short term, it may not be possible to meet the needs of the present without consuming resources, for example by burning oil or clearing areas of natural forest. Decision-makers have to consider the trade-off between different goals but, if the system as a whole is to survive, the use of natural assets must be compensated by the development of human or physical assets of equal or greater worth.

Good information is essential; that is, information about the needs of the people, about land resources and about the economic, social and environmental consequences of alternative decisions. The job of the land-use planner is to ensure that decisions are made on the basis of consensus or, failing that, informed disagreement.

In many cases, planning can reduce the costs in trade-off, for example by introducing appropriate new technology. It can also help to resolve conflict by involving the community in the planning process and by revealing the rationale and information on which decisions are based.

THE FOCUS OF LAND-USE PLANNING
Planning is for people

People's needs drive the planning process. Local farmers, other land users and the wider community who depend on the land must accept the need for a change in land use, as they will have to live with its results.

Land-use planning must be positive. The planning team must find out about people's needs and also the local knowledge, skills, labour and capital that they can contribute. It must study the problems of existing land-use practices and seek alternatives while drawing the public's attention to the hazards of continuing with present practices and to the opportunities for change.

Box 2
Acceptability – an example

Following the drought of 1973/74 and the subsequent famine, the Government of Ethiopia became more aware of the serious degradation of soil in the highlands.

An ambitious soil conservation programme has concentrated on protecting steep slopes by bunding and afforestation. This has made a substantial impact on soil erosion but has not contributed much to increased agricultural production. Large-scale afforestation is also unpopular with local people because it reduces the area available for livestock grazing while forest protection implies denying access for fuelwood collection. A balance between the competing requirements of conservation and production is clearly needed if popular support for soil conservation work is to continue without inducements such as the Food-for-Work Programme.

A land-use plan to conserve steeper slopes by restoring good vegetative cover through closure, followed by controlled grazing, has been found to be more acceptable to the local people than large-scale afforestation applied in isolation.

Regulations to prevent people doing what they now do for pressing reasons are bound to fail. Local acceptability is most readily achieved by local participation in planning. The support of local leaders is essential while the participation of agencies that have the resources to implement the plan is also important.

Land is not the same everywhere

Land is, self-evidently, the other focus of land-use planning. Capital, labour, management skills and technology can be moved to where they are needed. Land cannot be moved, and different areas present different opportunities and different management problems. Nor are land resources unchanging: this is obvious in the case of climate and vegetation, but examples such as the depletion of water resources or the loss of soil by erosion or salinity are reminders that resources can be degraded, in some cases irreversibly. Good information about land resources is thus essential to land-use planning.

Technology

A third element in planning is knowledge of land-use technologies: agronomy, silviculture, livestock husbandry and other means by which land is used. The technologies recommended must be those for which users have the capital, skills and other necessary resources; that is, appropriate technology. New technologies may have social and environmental implications that should be addressed by the planner.

Integration

A mistake in early attempts at land-use planning was to focus too narrowly on land resources without enough thought given to how they might be used. Good agricultural land is usually also suitable for other competing uses. Land-use decisions are not made just on the basis of land suitability but also according to the demand for products and the extent to which the use of a particular area is critical for a particular purpose. Planning has to integrate information about the suitability of the land, the demands for alternative products or uses

and the opportunities for satisfying those demands on the available land, now and in the future.

Therefore, land-use planning is not sectoral. Even where a particular plan is focused on one sector, e.g. smallholder tea development or irrigation, an integrated approach has to be carried down the line from strategic planning at the national level to the details of individual projects and programmes at district and local levels.

PLANNING AT DIFFERENT LEVELS

Land-use planning can be applied at three broad levels: national, district and local. These are not necessarily sequential but correspond to the levels of government at which decisions about land use are taken.

Different kinds of decision are taken at each level, where the methods of planning and kinds of plan also differ. However, at each level there is need for a land-use strategy, policies that indicate planning priorities, projects that tackle these priorities and operational planning to get the work done.

The greater the interaction between the three levels of planning, the better. The flow of information should be in both directions (Fig. 1). At each successive level of planning, the degree of

---

Box 3
Land-use regulations – a comment

The following observations, made by an FAO field staff member, could apply to almost any developing country:

• "There are a lot of regulations here – for example, forest conservation, fisheries – that are flouted with the connivance of the officials who are supposed to enforce them. Regulations have to be publicly accepted if they are to work. There aren't enough policemen to go around imposing unwanted regulations in rural areas."

• "Land-use planning is as much a matter of public education as of land-use zoning and regulation."

FIGURE 1
Two-way links between planning at different levels

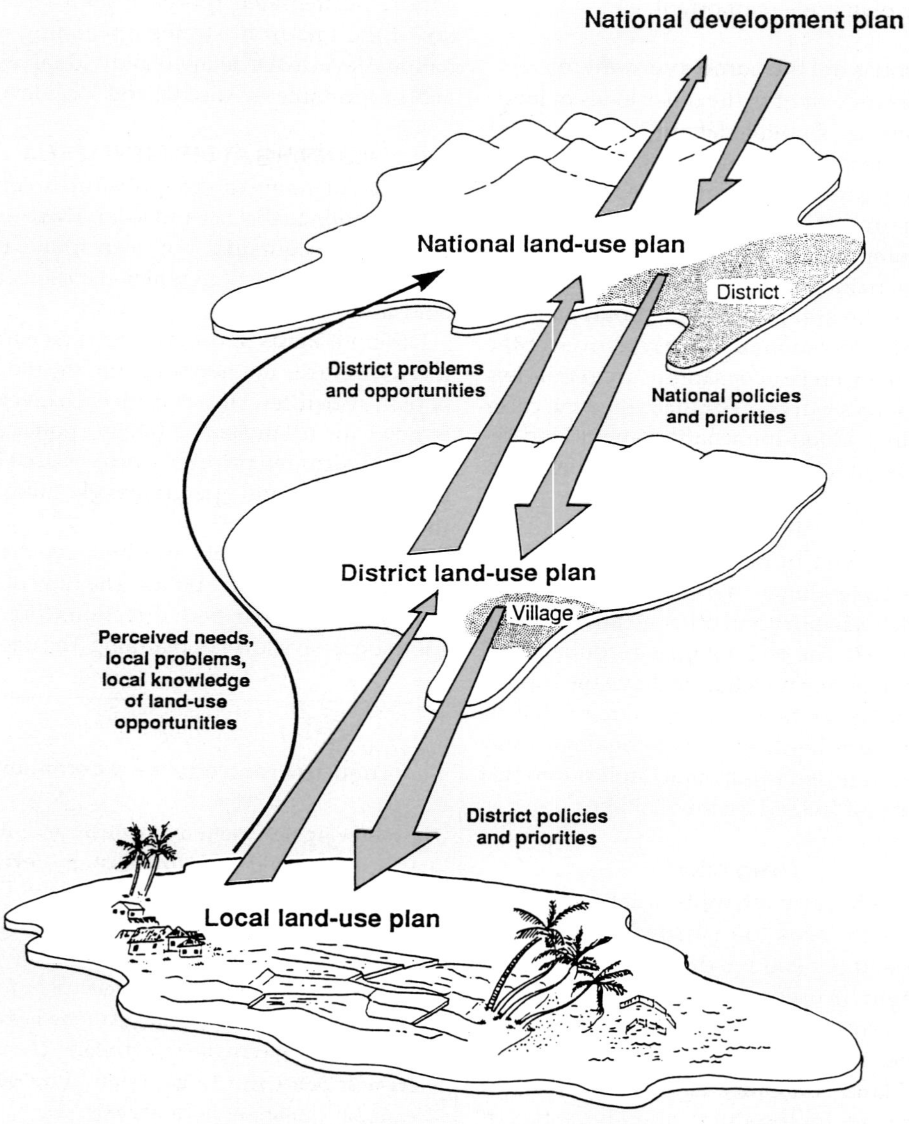

National development plan

National land-use plan

District

District problems
and opportunities

National policies
and priorities

District land-use plan

Village

Perceived needs,
local problems,
local knowledge
of land-use
opportunities

District policies
and priorities

Local land-use plan

detail needed increases, and so too should the direct participation of the local people.

National level

At the national level, planning is concerned with national goals and the allocation of resources. In many cases, national land-use planning does not involve the actual allocation of land for different uses, but the establishment of priorities for district-level projects. A national land-use plan may cover:

- land-use policy: balancing the competing demands for land among different sectors of the economy – food production, export crops, tourism, wildlife conservation, housing and public amenities, roads, industry;
- national development plans and budget: project identification and the allocation of resources for development;
- coordination of sectoral agencies involved in land use;
- legislation on such subjects as land tenure, forest clearance and water rights.

National goals are complex while policy decisions, legislation and fiscal measures affect many people and wide areas. Decision-makers cannot possibly be specialists in all facets of land use, so the planners' responsibility is to present the relevant information in terms that the decision-makers can both comprehend and act on.

District level

District level refers not necessarily to administrative districts but also to land areas that fall between national and local levels. Development projects are often at this level, where planning first comes to grips with the diversity of the land and its suitability to meet project goals. When planning is initiated nationally, national priorities have to be translated into local plans. Conflicts between national and local interests will have to be resolved. The kinds of issues tackled at this stage include:

- the siting of developments such as new settlements, forest plantations and irrigation schemes;
- the need for improved infrastructure such as water supply, roads and marketing facilities;
- the development of management guidelines for improved kinds of land use on each type of land.

Local level

The local planning unit may be the village, a group of villages or a small water catchment. At this level, it is easiest to fit the plan to the people, making use of local people's knowledge and contributions. Where planning is initiated at

---

Box 4
Starting at the local level: bottom-up planning

"Bottom-up" planning is initiated at the local level and involves active participation by the local community. The experience and local knowledge of the land users and local technical staff are mobilized to identify development priorities and to draw up and implement plans.

The advantages are:

- local targets, local management and local benefits. People will be more enthusiastic about a plan seen as their own, and they will be more willing to participate in its implementation and monitoring;
- more popular awareness of land-use problems and opportunities;
- plans can pay close attention to local constraints, whether these are related to natural resources or socio-economic problems;
- better information is fed upwards for higher levels of planning.

The disadvantages are that:

- local interests are not always the same as regional or national interests;
- difficulties occur in integrating local plans within a wider framework;
- limited technical knowledge at the local level means technical agencies need to make a big investment in time and labour in widely scattered places;
- local efforts may collapse because of a lack of higher-level support or even obstruction.

the district level, the programme of work to implement changes in land use or management has to be carried out locally. Alternatively, this may be the first level of planning, with its priorities drawn up by the local people. Local-level planning is about getting things done on particular areas of land – what shall be done where and when, and who will be responsible. Examples are:

- the layout of drainage, irrigation and soil conservation works;
- the design of infrastructure – road alignment and the siting of crop marketing, fertilizer distribution, milk collection or veterinary facilities;
- the siting of specific crops on suitable land.

Requests at the local level, e.g. for suitable areas to introduce tobacco or coffee, must be met with firm recommendations. For instance, "this land is suitable, this is not; these management practices are needed; it will cost so much and the expected returns are so much".

Planning at these different levels needs information at different scales and levels of generalization. Much of this information may be found on maps. The most suitable map scale for national planning is one by which the whole country fits on to one map sheet, which may call for a scale from 1:5 million to 1:1 million or larger. District planning requires details to be mapped at about 1:50 000, although some information may be summarized at smaller scales, down to 1:250 000.

For local planning, maps of between 1:20 000 and 1:5 000 are best. Reproductions of air photographs can be used as base maps at the local level, since field workers and experience show that local people can recognize where they are on the photos.

Land use in relation to sectoral and development planning

Land-use planning is non-sectoral by definition but, unless a special planning authority is set up, a plan must be implemented by sectoral agencies – in agriculture, forestry, irrigation, etc. Implementation will call for help from the different extension services.

There can be no clear boundary between land-use planning and other aspects of rural development. For example, a desirable change in land use may be the introduction of a cash crop. Successful management may require the use of fertilizer. This cannot be done unless there are local centres for fertilizer distribution, effective advice on its use and a system of credit for its purchase.

Local services will be of no use without an adequate national distribution system and the sufficient manufacture or allocation of foreign currency for imports. Building a fertilizer factory and organizing national distribution are certainly not part of land-use planning but they may be essential for the success of planned land use. On the other hand, the siting of local distribution centres in relation to population and suitable land could well be part of the work of a land-use planner.

Therefore, there is a spectrum of activities ranging from those that focus on the interpretation of the physical qualities of the land, for which the land-use planner will be largely responsible, to those that need a combined input

---

Box 5
Land-use, sectoral and integrated rural development plans

Land-use plans
- Allocate land to different kinds of land use;
- specify management standards and inputs;
- coordinate the work of sectoral agencies related to land use.

Sectoral plans
- These are projects and programmes of sectoral agencies, for example the forestry department and the irrigation department.

Integrated rural development plans
- Coordinate all aspects of rural development, including health, education, transport and land use.

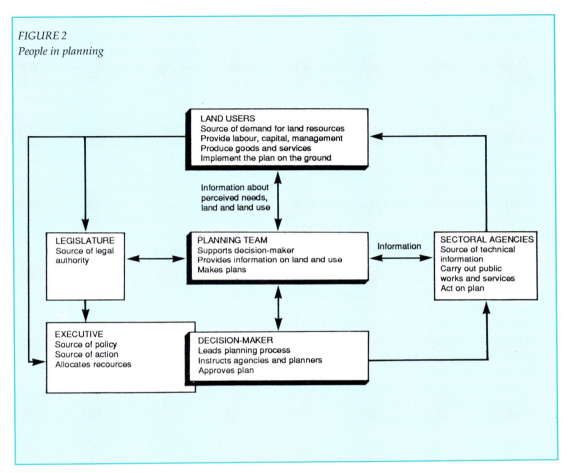

FIGURE 2
People in planning

with other technical specialists. Furthermore, where matters of national policy – adequate prices for crops, for example – are prerequisites for successful land use, the planner's job is to say so clearly.

People in planning

Land-use planning involves getting many different people to work together towards common goals. Three groups of people are directly involved (Fig. 2):

Land users. These are the people living in the planning area whose livelihood depends wholly or partly on the land. They include not only farmers, herders, foresters and others who use the land directly but also those who depend on these people's products, e.g. operators in crop or meat processing, sawmills and furniture factories. The involvement of all land users in planning is essential. Ultimately, they have to put the plan into effect and must therefore believe in its potential benefits as well as in the fairness of the planning process.

The experience and determination of local people in dealing with their environment are often the most neglected, as well as the most important, resource. People will grasp development opportunities that they themselves have helped to plan more readily than any that are imposed on them. Without the support of local leaders, a plan is not likely to succeed.

Achieving effective public participation in planning is a challenge. Planners have to invest the time and resources needed to secure partici-pation – through local discussions, by broad-casting and newspaper articles, through tech-nical workshops and extension services. Imagination, a sincere interest in people and the land as well as a willingness to experiment mark the more successful efforts.

Decision-makers. Decision-makers are those responsible for putting plans into effect. At national and district levels, they will usually be government ministers; at the local level, they will be members of the council or other authori-ties.

The planning team provides information and expert advice. The decision-makers guide the planning team on key issues and goals while also deciding whether to implement plans and, if so, which of the options presented should be chosen. Although the leader of the planning team is in charge of day-to-day planning activi-ties, the decision-maker should be involved at regular intervals.

Decision-makers also have a key role in en-couraging public participation through their willingness to expose their decisions and the way they are reached to public scrutiny.

The planning team. An essential feature of land-use planning is the treatment of land and land use as a whole. This involves crossing bound-aries between disciplines (natural resource, en-gineering, agricultural and social sciences), so teamwork is essential. Ideally, a team needs a wide range of special expertise; for example a soil surveyor, a land evaluation specialist, an agronomist, a forester, a range and livestock specialist, an engineer, an economist and a so-ciologist.

Such a range may only be available at the national level. At the local level, a more typical planning team may consist of a land-use plan-ner and one or two assistants. Each must tackle a wide range of jobs and will consequently need specialist advice. Government agency staff and universities may be useful sources of assistance.

APPLICATION

These guidelines are written in general terms, applicable to any environment or region. Many problems of land use are specific to particular areas, not only because of their differing physi-cal environments but also because of local so-cial conditions such as those of land tenure.

To acquire the feel of land-use planning, it is useful to read these guidelines in conjunction with examples of planning in practice. Thirteen such examples are assembled in the report, *Land-use planning applications. Proceedings of the FAO Expert Consultation 1990* (FAO, 1991b). Other accounts of land-use planning, including national handbooks and sources of examples, are listed in Chapter 4.

Chapter 2
Overview of the planning process

Every land-use planning project is different. Objectives and local circumstances are extremely varied, so each plan will require a different treatment. However, a sequence of ten steps has been found useful as a guide. Each step represents a specific activity, or set of activities, and their outputs provide information for subsequent steps.

Following is an outline of the steps which are described more fully in the next chapter (see also Figs 3 and 4).

Step 1. Establish goals and terms of reference. Ascertain the present situation; find out the needs of the people and of the government; decide on the land area to be covered; agree on the broad goals and specific objectives of the plan; settle the terms of reference for the plan.

Step 2. Organize the work. Decide what needs to be done; identify the activities needed and select the planning team; draw up a schedule of activities and outputs; ensure that everyone who may be affected by the plan, or will contribute to it, is consulted.

Step 3. Analyse the problems. Study the existing land-use situation, including in the field; talk to the land users and find out their needs and views; identify the problems and analyse their causes; identify constraints to change.

Step 4. Identify opportunities for change. Identify and draft a design for a range of land-use types that might achieve the goals of the plan; present these options for public discussion.

Step 5. Evaluate land suitability. For each promising land-use type, establish the land requirements and match these with the properties of the land to establish physical land suitability.

Step 6. Appraise the alternatives: environmental, economic and social analysis. For each physically suitable combination of land use and land, assess the environmental, economic and social impacts, for the land users and for the community as a whole. List the consequences, favourable and unfavourable, of alternative courses of action.

Step 7. Choose the best option. Hold public and executive discussions of the viable options and their consequences. Based on these discussions and the above appraisal, decide which changes in land use should be made or worked towards.

Step 8. Prepare the land-use plan. Make allocations or recommendations of the selected land uses for the chosen areas of land; make plans for appropriate land management; plan how the selected improvements are to be brought about and how the plan is to be put into practice; draw up policy guidelines, prepare a budget and draft any necessary legislation; involve decision-makers, sectoral agencies and land users.

Step 9. Implement the plan. Either directly within the planning process or, more likely, as a separate development project, put the plan into action; the planning team should work in conjunction with the implementing agencies.

Step 10. Monitor and revise the plan. Monitor the progress of the plan towards its goals; modify or revise the plan in the light of experience.

In a still broader view, the steps can be grouped into the following logical sequence:
- Identify the problems. *Steps 1-3.*
- Determine what alternative solutions exist. *Steps 4-6.*
- Decide which is the best alternative and prepare the plan. *Steps 7-8.*

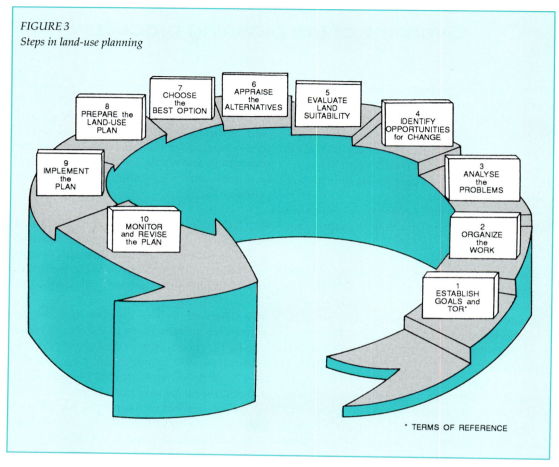

FIGURE 3

Steps in land-use planning

* TERMS OF REFERENCE

• Put the plan into action, see how it works and learn from this experience. *Steps 9-10.*

THE NEED FOR FLEXIBILITY

These steps, and the detailed procedures described under each, should not be followed rigidly. The circumstances of different land-use planning projects are highly varied and the guidelines presented here should be adapted to make the best of the local situation. What is important is to understand the purpose of each step or detailed procedure so that a decision can be made on whether it needs to be followed through, modified or omitted in the specific situation.

The above outline of steps and the descriptions that follow refer to the preparation of a

specific land-use plan in response to a perceived need. It is not always possible to work through the procedures step by step in this way. Two other approaches are possible: emergency planning and incremental planning.

Emergency planning

Land-use planners are often called in when a problem situation has already been identified, for example severe soil erosion or the onset of salinization in an irrigation scheme. An immediate diagnosis has to be made on the basis of a field visit and whatever information is to hand. Recommendations for remedial action are needed at once. In this situation, the planning process begins at Step 3, analysis of problems, and ends with a highly compressed version of

FIGURE 4
Steps in land-use planning: inputs, activities and outputs

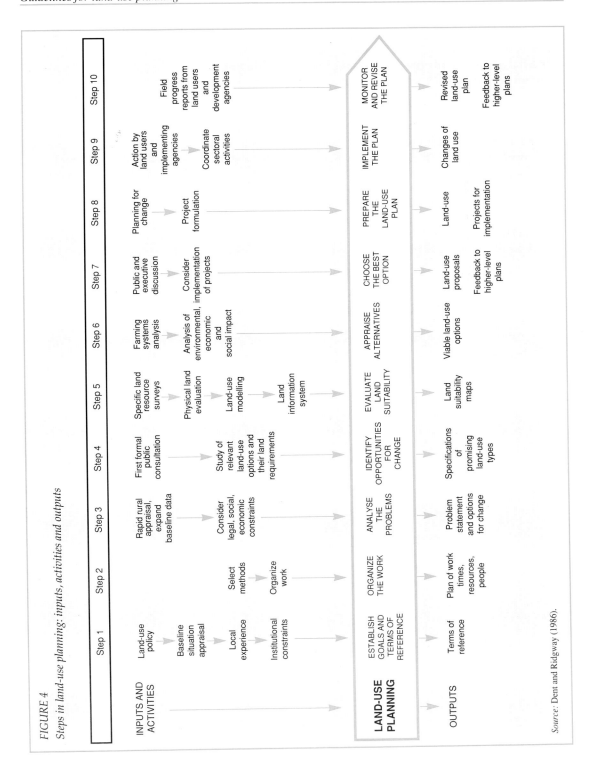

	Step 1	Step 2	Step 3	Step 4	Step 5	Step 6	Step 7	Step 8	Step 9	Step 10
INPUTS AND ACTIVITIES	Land-use policy	Rapid rural appraisal, expand baseline data	First formal public consultation	Specific land resource surveys	Farming systems analysis	Public and executive discussion	Planning for change	Action by land users and implementing agencies	Field progress reports from land users and development agencies
	Baseline situation appraisal			Physical land evaluation	Analysis of environmental, economic and social impact	Consider implementation of projects	Project formulation	Coordinate sectoral activities	
	Local experience	Select methods	Consider legal, social, economic constraints	Study of relevant land-use options and their land requirements	Land-use modelling				
	Institutional constraints	Organize work			Land information system				
LAND-USE PLANNING	ESTABLISH GOALS AND TERMS OF REFERENCE	ORGANIZE THE WORK	ANALYSE THE PROBLEMS	IDENTIFY OPPORTUNITIES FOR CHANGE	EVALUATE LAND SUITABILITY	APPRAISE ALTERNATIVES	CHOOSE THE BEST OPTION	PREPARE THE LAND-USE PLAN	IMPLEMENT THE PLAN	MONITOR AND REVISE THE PLAN
OUTPUTS	Terms of reference	Plan of work times, resources, people	Problem statement and options for change	Specifications of promising land-use types	Land suitability maps	Viable land-use options	Land-use proposals	Land-use	Changes of land use	Revised land-use plan
							Feedback to higher-level plans	Projects for implementation		Feedback to higher-level plans

Source: Dent and Ridgway (1986).

Steps 4 to 10. No general procedure can be offered but this kind of work needs an experienced team with a breadth of expertise in land resources, social sciences and the legal and administrative aspects of land use.

Incremental planning

Planning does not necessarily have to proceed by means of specific, time-bound plans. It can proceed incrementally, by making small local changes. An advantage is that mistakes, for example a crop variety that is attacked by a pest, can be identified early on before losses have become serious. This is how individual land users operate, but planners can also con-

tribute. They can assist change by offering their own skills, for example technical knowledge of small-scale irrigation methods, and by being agents in bringing in outside resources.

The initiative for incremental planning is likely to come from the land users (bottom-up planning). It requires that the planning agency should be on the spot and continuously in touch with the land users, and it is therefore more likely to be conducted by a national land-use planning agency or its district branches than by a specially convened external team. In formal terms this approach again commences with a perceived problem, Step 3, followed by a compressed version of Steps 4 to 10 in which

---

Box 6
Contents of the land-use plan

Executive summary. A summary of the goals, proposed changes in land use and methods for implementation of the plan, giving a clear overview of the essentials.

Terms of reference. Area, problems and goals (Step 1).

Land-use problems. Existing land-use systems and their problems (environmental, economic, social), constraints, environmental conservation standards (Step 3).

Land-use types and management. Improved systems of land use recommended for the area; how these should be managed on each land unit, for example drainage, crop varieties, tree species, fertilizer (Step 4).

Land suitability. Maps, tables and explanatory text showing the physical land suitability for each land-use type on each land unit (Step 5).

Appraisal of alternatives. Analysis of the environmental, economic and social consequences of alternative options for changes in land use (Step 6).

Recommended changes in land use. A statement on which changes in land use have been selected, together with reasons for these decisions (Step 7).

The land-use plan. Maps and text showing the selected changes in land use, and where they are to be implemented or recommended (Step 8).

Implementation of the plan. How the planned improvements are to be put into practice; requirements for staffing, training, extension, infrastructure, supplies, research; timing and budget (Step 8).

Procedures for monitoring and revision. How the degree of success of the plan is to be assessed; procedures for ongoing revision (Step 10).

Supporting information. Detailed information gathered in the course of the planning exercise (for example rainfall variability, soil survey, forest inventory, population data, maps and statistics of present land use, study of marketing facilities, summary of interviews with farmers). This is so that people can understand the reasons for decisions taken and, where appropriate, re-evaluate selected aspects in the light of changes in circumstances.

one or more solutions to the problem are identified, their consequences considered and action taken.

PLANNING AND IMPLEMENTATION

Plans are made in order to be put into practice; the effort put into the planning exercise is wasted if this is not done. Occasionally, the outcome of the planning process may be a recommendation that changes are undesirable or impracticable but, normally, successful implementation marks the achievement of the goals of the plan.

In most cases, however, implementation is not part of the planning process as such, but is a separate exercise. Step 8 prepares for implementation while Step 10 is the planning activity which continues in parallel with it. In these guidelines, the description of Step 9 is an account of the potential roles of the planning team in implementation.

At the national level, implementation is usually a matter of government decisions on priorities. In planning at the district level, implementation will often be achieved through a development project, requiring considerably greater resources of personnel and finance than the planning exercise. In this circumstance, Steps 8 and 9 are effectively a pre-project evaluation. It is only at the local level that implementation may be more integral with planning, using the same team and resources.

PLANNING AS AN ITERATIVE PROCESS

Planning has to be continuous. There is never enough knowledge about the land and its response to management and, as more information and experience are gained, plans have to be changed. Figures 3 and 4 show the planning process progressing in logical steps, one after another, although in practice it is often necessary to repeat earlier steps in the light of experience. In particular, the land-use proposals arrived at by Step 7 should be open to discussion and may be recast several times by repeating earlier steps of the planning process before a firm choice is made and the plan implemented.

Further changes may be needed during the lifetime of a plan because external conditions change, for example the development of new markets for a product or a change of government policy.

The planner's task is never finished! Some of the changes in land use may have proved unsuccessful. Frequently, changes that were desirable five, ten or 20 years ago are no longer suited to present circumstances. The circular or iterative nature of land-use planning suggested in Figure 3 has an element of truth in it; a time may come when monitoring and revision of a previous plan is no longer sufficient and the planners will need to shift from Step 10 of an earlier plan to Step 1 of a new one.

THE LAND-USE PLAN

The planning exercise will normally be presented as a report with maps. For more substantial plans, the report is likely to consist of a relatively short executive summary; a main text volume, with maps, describing the changes proposed; and one or more volumes of appendixes giving supporting data. An outline of what the report is likely to contain is given in Box 6, Contents of the land-use plan, which indicates the steps that have contributed to each section.

Chapter 3
Steps in land-use planning

This section sets out the tasks involved in making a land-use plan following the ten steps outlined in the previous chapter. For each step it gives:
- the objectives, i.e. why the step is needed;
- the main activities included;
- the information to be collected and its sources;
- the people involved and their responsibilities.

Each step is summarized by means of a *Checklist*.

Further details of methods available, with sources which can be consulted for details, are given in Chapter 4. An aspect common to all of the steps is that of "information management" (see Chapter 4, p. 75, and Glossary).

As already emphasized, these steps should be treated as guidelines to be adapted to the circumstances of specific plans.

Step 1

ESTABLISH GOALS AND TERMS OF REFERENCE

Getting started

The planning effort is launched by discussions between those who want the plan (land users and government) and the planners. This crucial first step should be a mutual exchange of ideas and information.

The decision-makers and representatives of the people of the planning area have to brief the planner about the problems of the area and what they want to achieve. The planner has to make clear how a land-use plan might help. A reconnaissance field tour, during which representatives of the people concerned are met, can be especially useful.

The planning assignment

The following tasks may be included in this first step of planning. Some of them will be repeated in more detail in Steps 3 and 4.

- *Define the planning area.* Determine and map its location, size, boundaries, access and centres of population.

- *Contact the people involved.* Before any decisions are taken, representatives of the farmers and other land users likely to be affected by the plan should be contacted and their views obtained. This serves two purposes: first, it provides the planning team with an inside view of the real situation; second, it means that the land users are aware that changes are being considered instead of being confronted with them subsequently as something imposed from above. Make sure that all groups of people are contacted, including women's organizations, ethnic minorities, pastoralists as well as cultivators. Particular attention should be given to ways in which minorities depend on land resources, e.g. through the collection of minor forest products.

- *Acquire basic information about the area.* This is a first stage of gathering information which will be acquired in more detail in later steps. It is needed at this point to establish what the plan is intended to achieve. The kinds of information needed are outlined in Basic information about the area (p. 18).

• *Establish the goals.* The goals may arise from local problems (e.g. low crop yields, fodder shortages) or from national policy and development priorities (e.g. crops for export). At any particular level, the goals may have been derived from higher levels (from national to district and local) or lower levels (by the amalgamation of local needs) – top-down and bottom-up planning, respectively. List the problems of the area and the benefits sought; distinguish between long-term goals and those that can be achieved in the planning period; isolate those goals of higher-level plans that apply to the area and those that do not.

• *Identify the problems and opportunities.* Illustrate the present land-use situation. Identify the problems that the plan is intended to tackle and the opportunities for improvement.

• *Identify constraints to implementation.* Constraints to the implementation of the proposed plan may be legal, economic, institutional, social or environmental. The design of any interventions must explicitly recognize the capacity of government, other organizations and land users to implement them. The resources available must be specified.

• *Establish the criteria by which land-use decisions will be made.* For example, the option chosen may be the one which promises the highest return on investment, or the one which will sustain the greatest rural population. Where there are several criteria, decide on their relative importance.

• *Set the scope of the plan.* How much is the plan supposed to cover? Will other plans still be in effect? For example, will roads or other basic services be covered by the plan?

• *Set the planning period.* This is the length of time for which the plan will operate. It could be three or five years or longer, and may be broken down into phases for review and revision.

• *Agree on the content and format of the plan.* What will the plan contain? How will it be presented? For example, will it include new crops, improved techniques of land management, extension services, improvements in infrastructure or new legislation? The format depends on the people who have to be informed and involved; identify the different groups of people concerned.

• *Decide operational questions.* These include the funding of the planning operation, the authority and organization of the team, facilities, cooperation with other agencies, record-keeping and reporting arrangements, key people who can help or who need to be informed and the plan's production schedule.

Basic information about the area

To get started, the planning team will need some basic information about the land, the people and the organization of administration and services. This information will be obtained in more detail in the analysis of problems in Step 3. In Step 1, the planner must find out what is available and where to get it, and must identify the people who can serve as contacts between the planning team, specialist agencies and the local community. The planner must also find out which essential data are not available, so that surveys can be scheduled and costed. The range of information and amount of detail needed will vary according to the level of planning. Following are examples of information that may be required:

• *Land resources.* Climate, hydrology, geology, landforms, soils, vegetation (including forest and pasture resources), fauna, pests and diseases. Sources include topographic base maps, air photographs and satellite imagery, existing surveys and departmental records. (See Natural resource surveys, p. 78)

- *Present land use.* Surveys and departmental records of land use, farming systems, forestry, production levels and trends.
- *Present infrastructure.* Transport, communication and services to agriculture, livestock management and forestry.
- *Population.* Numbers, demographic trends, location of settlements, the role of women, ethnic groups, class structure, leadership.
- *Land tenure.* Legal and traditional ownership and user rights for land, trees and grazing; forest reserves, national parks. (See Land tenure, p. 81)
- *Social structure and traditional practices.* Land use is tied up with the history and culture of the people and has usually evolved over a long period. Understanding the present situation is a prerequisite for devising improvements.
- *Government.* Administrative structure and key authorities; services provided and demands placed upon them. Ask representatives of the various agencies active in the area to brief the planning team.
- *Legislation.* Laws and regulations that affect land use; traditional law and custom; whether laws are enforced. (See Legislation for land use, p. 81.)
- *Non-governmental organizations (NGOs).* Find out about NGOs in the planning area, for example farming and marketing cooperatives, that may have roles in planning or implementing a land-use plan.
- *Commercial organizations.* Contact any commercial organizations, e.g. mining companies, whose interests may be affected.

essential to develop close working relationships between the land users, the decision-makers, the planning team and other participants of the planning process.

A major requirement of this step is to identify the main components of the planning project. From these, the terms of reference should be defined broadly enough to allow flexibility in finding solutions to the land-use problems identified while staying within the limits of the time and resources available.

The output from this step will be a project document (or similar statement) giving the terms of reference of the planning exercise, including its goals, specific objectives, time required and the necessary budget.

Terms of reference and budget

Step 1 is the foundation of the land-use plan. Misconceptions arising at this stage may be difficult to clear up later. In particular, it is

CHECKLIST

Step 1

GOALS AND TERMS OF REFERENCE

Responsibility: decision-makers and planners together

❏ Define the planning area.

❏ Contact the people involved.

❏ Acquire basic information about the area:
  − land resources
  − present land use
  − infrastructure
  − population
  − land tenure
  − social structure
  − government
  − NGOs
  − commercial organizations

❏ Establish the goals.

❏ Make a preliminary identification of problems and opportunities.

❏ Identify constraints to implementing improvements.

❏ Establish the criteria for making decisions on land use.

❏ Set the scope of the plan.

❏ Set the planning period.

❏ Agree on the content and format of the plan.

❏ Decide on operational questions for the planning project: personnel, cooperating agencies, timing, budget.

Step 2

ORGANIZE THE WORK

What the work plan does

Work planning is not exciting. If it is not done thoroughly, however, the consequences can be a lack of coordination, frustration and needless delays. Of course, unpredictable events will occur but good organization can forestall many problems and help everyone to work together by focusing their energies.

This step transforms the general planning procedure from Step 1 into a specific programme of work. It says what needs to be done, decides on the methods, identifies who will do it, specifies the responsibilities of each team member, schedules personnel and activities and allocates resources for the ensuing steps in the planning process.

Why is it needed?

Coordination of the very diverse activities involved in land-use planning is important because:

- *Many tasks have a long lead time.* For example, gathering information must begin as early as possible – some surveys take many months to complete.
- *Supporting services must be organized;* for example, transport, labour, cartography, printing. These must be scheduled so they

---

FIGURE 5
Example of phasing project work using a bar chart

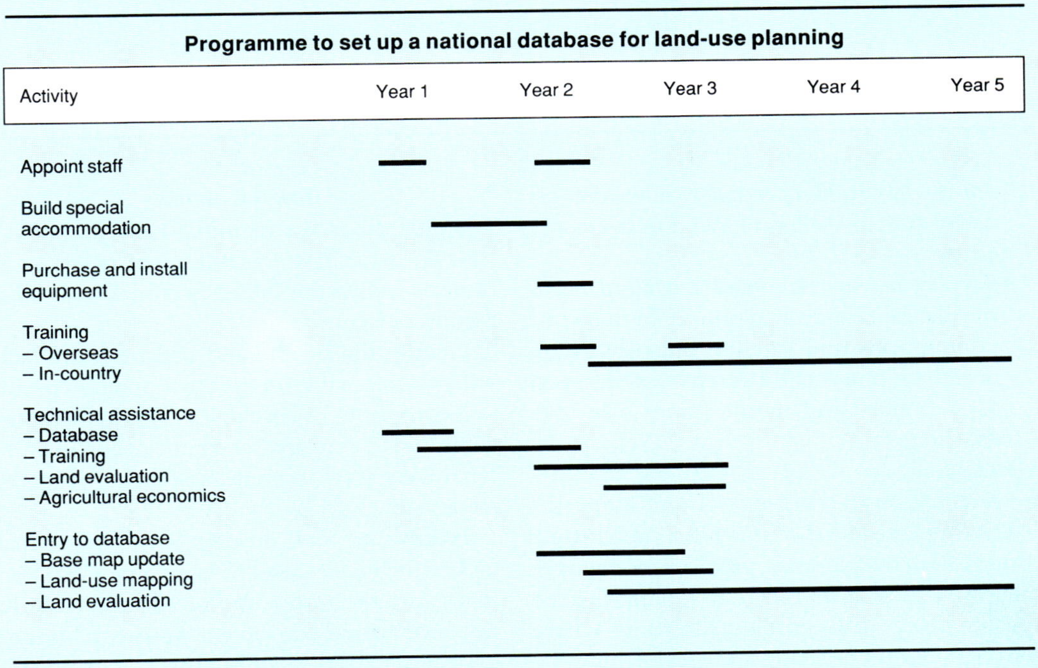

Programme to set up a national database for land-use planning

Activity	Year 1	Year 2	Year 3	Year 4	Year 5

Appoint staff

Build special
accommodation

Purchase and install
equipment

Training
– Overseas
– In-country

Technical assistance
– Database
– Training
– Land evaluation
– Agricultural economics

Entry to database
– Base map update
– Land-use mapping
– Land evaluation

TABLE 1
Example of a planning table

	Sen Gong District Land-use Plan			
Planning step	Task	Resources	Responsibility	Due date
1. First meeting	Identify participants	Director, decision-maker	J. Cruz	01/09/87
	Assemble materials	Agency library, five-year plan, National database	E.J. Evans	15/09/87
	Arrange venue, support staff, transport	Administration unit, motor pool	M. Wong	30/09/87
3. Structure problems and opportunities	Develop questionnaire	Regional statistician, consultant on public involvement	S. Moe (with J.E. Hoover)	01/02/88
3.1. Problem statements	Identify and interview key people	Contact list, interview forms, team vehicle, field assistant	T.F. Guy	20/03/88
	Prepare problem statements	Interview data	T.F. Guy S. Moe	01/04/88
3.2. Find options for change	Set benchmarks	Land resources survey (1985), district agronomist, team vehicle	S. Moe (with M. Wong)	05/05/88
	Summarize regulations	Agency code book, law clerk	F. Sims	30/05/88

are available when needed, to make the best use of staff as well as to avoid unnecessary costs.

• *Supplies and materials must be obtained.* Security clearance may be required for maps, air photographs and satellite imagery. More mundane but equally essential items such as stationery and motor spares also take time to get.

• *Training, travel, review meetings and consultancies must be scheduled* months ahead. The time of trained staff is often the greatest constraint in the planning project. Good judgement is needed at this stage in identifying the specific needs of the project, deciding where short cuts might be made and establishing the need for particular activities and information.

How is it done?

First, list the major planning tasks and activities. For each task, outline what needs to be done as well as the skilled personnel and other resources required.

Identify the people and organizations who will be responsible for each task and others who will contribute. A checklist of jobs and responsibilities is a priority. Everyone needs to know what is expected of them and to whom they are responsible.

Specify the time needed to complete each task, which tasks need to be completed before others can be started and the deadlines. Allocate money and equipment. Draw up budgets for each activity and list the resources (e.g. transport, equipment) that will be needed.

FIGURE 6
Example of a critical path chart

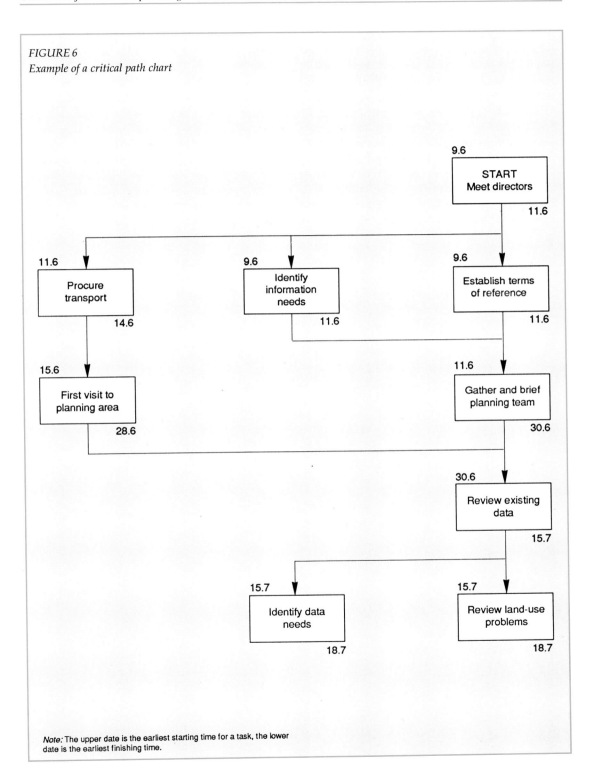

Note: The upper date is the earliest starting time for a task, the lower date is the earliest finishing time.

The simplest format for the work plan is a table, as shown in Table 1. This can be expanded to include locations of activities, materials required, times taken, budget figures and details of output such as reports and maps.

A bar chart is a clear way of displaying the work plan (Fig. 5). Colouring in the bars as each stage is completed highlights whether the work is keeping to schedule. If the project is large and complex, a critical path chart can be drawn up (Fig. 6). This is based on the concept of a preceding activity, a task which has to be completed before another can be started. Such a chart draws attention to what the key activities are, where delays will slow down the project as a whole.

However, land-use planning projects must be allowed to evolve. Not all activities can be foreseen and timed in advance, especially in situations involving several independent organizations with different workloads. A critical path analysis is not appropriate for an evolving planning project with a time frame extending over several years, but the discipline of producing a work plan of this kind for each individual step of the process can be valuable.

CHECKLIST

Step 2

ORGANIZATION OF THE WORK

Responsibility: planning team leader and administrator

❏ List the planning tasks and activities. For each task:
  – identify the people and organizations responsible for or contributing to it;
  – set out the resources needed;
  – estimate the time needed.

❏ Decide which tasks need to be completed before others can be commenced.

❏ Draw up a work plan for the project as a whole (table, bar chart or critical path analysis).

❏ Draw up individual, personal work plans.

❏ Allocate money and equipment.

❏ Arrange administrative matters and logistics:
  – Check and arrange security clearances for staff and equipment, e.g. for the purchase and use of maps, air photographs and computers.
  – Budget for staff, equipment and transport costs.
  – Provide for:
    • transport (vehicles, spares, fuel, servicing);
    • equipment;
    • office facilities.
  – Provide and coordinate technical support:
    • inputs from other agencies
    • field assistance
    • laboratory
    • cartography
    • secretarial
  – Make provision for wet or hot seasons, public and local holidays, contingencies and iteration of steps in the planning process.

Step 3

ANALYSE THE PROBLEMS

After the previous focus on discussion, terms of reference and preparation, Step 3 is the first to involve the detailed technical aspects of land-use planning. It is a big step. First, the existing land-use situation has to be analysed and compared with the development goals; to do this requires the identification of land units and land-use systems. Next, problems with the present land use must be identified, including their nature and severity. Finally, the causes of these problems must be analysed.

The existing situation

In Step 1, some basic facts about the area were assembled. Now it is necessary to gather information on the existing situation in much more detail, to provide the factual basis for all subsequent steps, up to implementation. Much of this information should be shown on maps.

Assuming that data on the administrative structure, legal framework and interested organizations has been gathered in Step 1, the information now needed includes:

- *Population.* Analyse the numbers, age and sex structure, population trends and distribution. Plot these data – towns, villages and dispersed rural settlements – on the base map.
- *Land resources.* Obtain, compile or, where necessary, survey land resource data relevant to the planning task. This may include landforms, climate, agroclimatic regions, soils, vegetation, pasture resources, forests and wildlife. (See Natural resource surveys, p. 78.)
- *Employment and income.* Summarize data by area, age, social and ethnic groups.
- *Present land use.* Existing information will often be out of date or unreliable. Make an up-to-date land-use map. This is an essential basis for planning changes.
- *Production and trends.* Tabulate production data; graph production trends and eco-nomic projections for the planning period. This information should be as quantitative as possible.
- *Infrastructure.* Plot roads, market and service centres on the base map.

Most of this information will be obtained from existing sources, supplemented by field reconnaissance to check how up to date and reliable these are. Gaps of importance may need filling in by methods of rapid rural appraisal, remote sensing and field surveys as well as talking with people who know the area, e.g. agricultural or forestry extension staff.

Land units and land-use systems. To analyse the present situation it will be necessary to break the area down into *land units*, areas that are relatively homogeneous with respect to climate, landforms, soils and vegetation. Each land unit presents similar problems and opportunities and will respond in similar ways to management.

Appropriate land units at the national level might be *agroclimatic regions*; at the district level, *land systems*; and, at the local level, *land facets*, *soil series* or other *soil mapping units*.

The next step is to identify the more common *land-use systems*, areas with similar land use and economy. These may be *farming systems* or systems based on forestry, etc. Land-use systems are frequently defined in terms of dominant crops, e.g. a maize/tobacco system. Other common criteria for differentiating land-use systems within a land unit are large and small farms or those with and without livestock.

One practical difficulty is that neither land units nor land-use systems will correspond to the administrative units for which economic and population data are usually available and by which many planning decisions are taken. There is no easy solution: planners have to work simultaneously with land units, land-use systems and administrative units.

PLATE 3
A village meeting. Meetings in the field with representatives of those involved help the planner see problems from the people's point of view. They also alert the people to the fact that changes are being considered. Farmers and other land users should be consulted and their views obtained from the earliest stages of plan preparation right through to its implementation – without their willing acceptance and help, no plan can succeed

TABLE 2

Land-use problems: symptoms and causes

SYMPTOMS OF LAND-USE PROBLEMS

Migration to towns
Low rural incomes
Lack of employment opportunities
Poor health and nutrition
Inadequate subsistence production
Shortage of fuel and timber
Shortage of grazing land
Low, unreliable crop yields
Desertion of farmland
Encroachment on forest and wildlife reserves
Conflicts among farming, livestock and non-agricultural uses
Visible land degradation, e.g. eroded cropland, silted
   bottomlands, degradation of woodland, salinity in irrigation
   schemes, flooding

UNDERLYING CAUSES RELATED TO LAND USE

Social problems
Population pressure on land resources
Unequal distribution of land, capital and opportunities
Restrictions of land tenure and landownership

Natural hazards and limitations
Inadequate water supply and distribution
Irregular relief
Drought-prone soils
Poor drainage
Diseases

Mismatch between land use and land suitability
Inadequate water control
Clearance of forest on steeplands
Inadequate soil conservation practices
Inadequate periods of bush fallow

Related rural planning problems
Inadequate power
Lack of fertilizer and pesticides
Lack of markets, unsatisfactory price structure
Lack of finance
Inadequate transport
Lack of technical support

Problems of land use

To define a problem it is necessary to establish the present situation, judge ways in which it is unsatisfactory and identify ways in which it might be made better.

Apart from when planning new settlements on unoccupied land, this stage of diagnosis of problems is of the highest importance. Without identifying problems and analysing their causes, one is in no position to plan for improving the situation. Three closely related methods, any of which can be used at this stage, are *farming systems analysis, diagnosis and design* and *rapid*

rural appraisal (see Rural land-use analysis, p. 79).

The fundamental field survey method may be summarized as:
- talk to the people;
- look at the land.

"People" include the farmers and other land users, local leaders, extension staff and agencies active in the area. Where time allows, a set of interviews should be conducted with farmers sampled from each land-use system. Table 2 gives some examples of problems of land-use systems. Identify which are considered to be the most important – by the farmers, by local agencies and by the planning team.

At the same time, diagnose the causes of the problems identified. For example, a fodder shortage may be caused by cultivation encroaching on former grazing land, coupled with a lack of rotational grazing and/or control of livestock numbers on the latter. The effects may be indirect: a labour shortage on farms at a critical period might be made worse by the fact that women have to travel long distances to collect fuelwood or water.

Field observation is complementary to interviews. Ask to be shown around farms and travel about the area. This will reveal physical problems such as soil erosion, overgrazing and forest degradation.

Taking present land use as the basis, ask:
- How is the land managed now?
- What will happen if the present management continues unchanged?
- Why is it the way it is? Is it the best available system of land use or is it followed because of tradition, insufficient labour, lack of capital, a need for staple food, a need for cash, a need for time for communal activities and leisure, a desire to retain landownership, a lack of skill or technical knowledge or poor planning?

Group together issues that seem to be related. Try to distinguish between symptoms and underlying causes. For example, the direct cause of a food shortage may be declining yields; these result from cultivation without fallow

Plate 4
A fuelwood shortage: a simplified example of a problem statement

The problem. A severe fuelwood shortage affects small farms in this land unit. Women spend many hours each day gathering and carrying wood. Surveys show a one-third decrease in tree cover over the past five years.
Causes. The shortage has developed as a result of greater demand, caused by increased population and leading to prolonged cutting of natural woodland. There is no extension programme to tell people about growing trees.
Opportunities for change. There are two opportunities to improve this situation: i) the establishment of fuelwood plantations, managed by the local community, on lower slopes of adjacent hills; ii) growing trees on farms, using agroforestry technologies such as boundary planting.

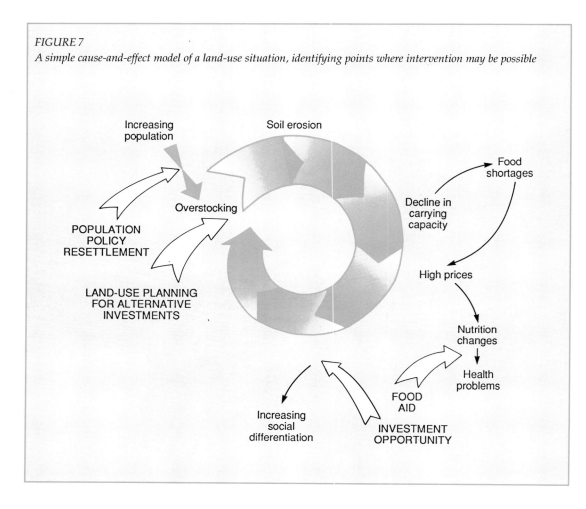

FIGURE 7

A simple cause-and-effect model of a land-use situation, identifying points where intervention may be possible

which, in turn, is caused by a land shortage coupled with increasing population.

Problems can sometimes be modelled. Models may range from cause-and-effect linkages (Fig. 7) to quantitative simulations or economic models. Models help to show linkages in the land-use system and may help to identify possible opportunities for change (see Modelling, p. 79 and Systems analysis, p. 77).

Separate problems that can be tackled by local land-use planning from those that are beyond its scope. For example, it is no use encouraging production of a bulky export crop if there is no road to the coast.

Problem statements

This stage can be summarized by a set of *problem statements* which, for each problem, give:
- its nature and severity with respect to land units and land-use systems;
- its short-term and long-term effects;
- a summary of its causes: physical, economic and social.

CHECKLIST

Step 3

ANALYSIS OF PROBLEMS

Responsibility: planning team

❏ Collect data on the existing situation; where possible, compile maps:
  – population;
  – land resources;
  – employment and income;
  – present land use;
  – production and trends;
  – infrastructure.

❏ *Sources:* maps, satellite imagery, air photographs, censuses, departmental records. Check in the field whether the sources are reliable and up to date.

❏ Identify and map:
  – land units;
  – land-use systems.

❏ Identify problems of land use:
  – nature and severity, land units and land-use systems affected;
  – analysis of causes.

❏ *Methods:* interviews with land users, local leaders, extension staff, agencies; field reconnaissance.

❏ Prepare problem statements.

Step 4

IDENTIFY OPPORTUNITIES FOR CHANGE

Now that the problems needing attention are known, the next step is to consider what can be done to solve or ameliorate them. This requires interaction between the planning team, which devises and presents its alternative opportunities for change, the land users, who comment on these opportunities and may offer their own solutions and the decision-makers, who choose which alternatives are to be analysed further.

Seek a variety of solutions in the first instance, then select those that seem most promising. All reasonable solutions should be considered in Step 4 because it becomes increasingly difficult to follow new directions as planning progresses. It is important for the land users, planners and decision-makers to reach a consensus about what the priorities are, and this entails both public involvement and wide-ranging executive discussion.

Opportunities

Planning involves seeking and appraising opportunities for closing the gap between the present situation and the goals. Opportunities are presented by untapped human and land resources, new technology and economic or political circumstances.

The people present opportunities in the form of labour, skills and culture and, not least, the ability to adjust to change and to survive adversity. Cooperation at the local level may be promoted by encouraging the participation of land-use groups in the planning process and through buyer and producer organizations.

The land may have underdeveloped regions or unexploited resources such as water power, economic minerals or scenery and wildlife. The location of the planning area may give it a strategic advantage for trade or defence. The

---

Box 7
Identification of options for solving a problem

Existing situation:[*] chronic food shortage, accelerating degradation of grazing land.

Specification for improved land use: increase rural income, arrest land degradation.

Options
- Non-land-use planning options – emigration or, in the long term, birth control.
- Do-nothing policy, which means accelerating land degradation and increasing dependence on food aid; therefore rejected.
- A sustainable increase in production might be achieved by:
  - the control of stock numbers combined with rotational grazing, allowing herbage to recover;
  - a combination of controlled grazing and improved forage production by top-dressing, re-

seeding and physical soil conservation measures to increase infiltration of rainfall;
  - the supplementary feeding of stock during critical periods, using either imported forage or conserved forage grown locally with the use of irrigation.
- These options merely control the livestock problem. Some alternatives are needed that will alleviate the shortage of food and fuel. Therefore, consider:
  - the diversification of land use by combining livestock, crops and possibly fuelwood production by agroforestry, for example.

For any of these options to be implemented, there must be a reform of land tenure and grazing rights that is acceptable to the community as a whole.

_____
[*] The land-use situation (problem) is illustrated in Figure 7.

land nearly always has the potential for greater or more diverse production, given investment in management.

New crops and land uses may be available. Circumstances may have changed so much, e.g. through population growth, that it is no longer possible to solve problems by improving the existing land use. A completely new use may be necessary, e.g. irrigation.

Improved technology can transform the productive potential of the land – for example fertilizers, pesticides, improved drainage or irrigation practices, new ways to store or process products, improved crop and livestock varieties. Research and extension services play key roles in developing, adapting and introducing new technology.

Economic opportunities include new sources of capital, new or improved markets, changes to the price structure, the improvement of transport and communications. Often, the application of improved technology to land is rendered difficult or impossible by the relative prices of inputs and products.

Government action may create opportunities, for example by the reform of land tenure and administrative structure and through policies of taxation, pricing, subsidies and investment.

At this stage, the opportunities considered need not be specified in great detail but should be wide-ranging to include all possibilities that appear realistic (a process sometimes called "brainstorming").

Options for change

There is usually more than one way to tackle a problem. Alternatives may be needed to give due attention to the interests of competing groups and serve as a starting point for negotiations. The plan that is finally accepted may include aspects of more than one option.

The options developed in this step will depend on the goals, the strategy pursued to reach these goals, opportunities and problems presented by the people and the land and the finance and other resources available. For example, problems of food production will demand agricultural or economic action; opportunities for tourism will depend on ways of attracting and accommodating tourists.

Options can be described in terms of ways and means:

- *Non-land-use planning options.* In the example illustrated by Figure 7, population policy and food aid are beyond the scope of land-use planning.

- *Allocations of land use.* Land-use types are allocated to specific areas of land; for example, irrigated farming to bottomlands, forestry to steep slopes and stream reservations. This option is widely applied in new settlement schemes but is more difficult to apply where land is already occupied.

- *New land uses.* A complete change is made by introducing new kinds of land use not previously practised in the area, for example irrigation.

- *Improvements to land-use types.* Improvements are made to existing farming systems or other land-use types in order to make them more productive or sustainable. The improvements must be brought about through extension services, often combined with improved infrastructure and services (e.g. supplies of inputs). This option follows directly from the analysis of problems. It is one of the principal means of bringing about change in areas that have already been settled.

- *Standards.* Standards may consist of planning guidelines or limits. For example, conservation standards might specify "no cultivation within 40 m of streams or on slopes greater than 12°"; limits to safeguard life and property might specify "no housing or industrial development in designated flood hazard or landslide zones". Standards of this kind, however, are hard to enforce, unless the problems that have led to their being broken are addressed.

Other standards refer to land management, for example standards for terrace construction, fertilization or land drainage. Interest rates on loans for farm improvement may be limited, to 5 percent for instance. For subsequent land evaluation, these management standards are built into the defined land-use types.

Procedures

There is no fixed procedure for selection of alternatives for change. Some courses of action will be suggested by farmers, others by extension staff or people with an interest in the area, while the planners may develop still others from the information obtained in Step 3. What is essential is to keep all interested people informed and seek their views. Some guidelines are as follows:

- *Focus on questions regarding what action can be taken within the plan.* Some decisions may have been made already at a higher level of planning. For example, it may have been decided at the national level to build a road through the planning area. The choice to be made locally is the route, based on how it will best serve the existing or planned settlements.

- *Consider alternative land-use strategies.* None of the following strategies are likely to be followed alone. They represent extremes to be used as a basis for an analysis and comparison of different courses of action.
  - *No change.* Continue the present systems of land use. Since there are problems, this is unlikely to be adopted, but examination of its consequences is useful to see if suggested improvements are any better.
  - *Maximum production.* This may be for all products, for selected products (e.g. food crops), for maximum financial benefit or to support the greatest number of people on the land.
  - *Minimum public investment.* To bring about

improvements which benefit the people while making the lowest demands on scarce investment funds.
  - *Maximum conservation.* Maximum production in the short term may lead to accelerating erosion or pollution. The alternative of maximum conservation may be costly or may imply a lower level of production.
  - *Maximum equity.* A deliberate attempt to give added benefits to poorer sections of the community or to minority groups.

- *Identify a range of possible solutions.* Options may be built around various themes. The planner must find the theme that is most relevant to the goals and the planning area. Again, a compromise between extremes will be necessary.
  - *Types of production.* Which type of production should be encouraged: commercial, subsistence or a combination of the two? How should land and resources be allocated between the different kinds of production?
  - *Production or conservation?* A trade-off between these alternatives is often necessary in the short term. Standards, and hence allocation of land to different uses, may differ between these alternatives. For example, the maximum slope angle of cultivated land may be 20° in the "production" alternative and 8° in the "conservation" alternative.
  - *Self-reliance or outside investment?* An alternative favouring self-reliance would be based on traditional crops, intermediate technology and local credit. An alternative requiring outside assistance might introduce more sophisticated technology, perhaps new crops and outside finance.

Identify a wide range of possible solutions that meet each of the demands in the planning area. For example, if a shortage of fuelwood is a problem, then all the land not already cultivated could be put into fuelwood plantations, even though much of the area is grazed and there is also a shortage of pasture. Alternatively, fuel could be imported, if this is feasible, without planning for any change in fuelwood production.

• *Develop options within the extremes.* Develop options that have a realistic chance of being implemented. Moderate the maximum range of options by social imperatives, budgetary and administrative constraints, the demands of competing land uses and an initial assessment of land suitability. Thus, the planner addressing the fuelwood and grazing problems might develop three options: to allocate 20 percent of the area to fuelwood plantations, retain 30 percent of the area in grazing and import fuel to meet the continuing but reduced need; to meet the fuelwood demand by having 30 percent of the area under plantations, with a reduction in pasture; or the same as the second option, but with a parallel extension effort in intensive livestock production to compensate for the reduction in grazing area.

Compatible land uses can be combined to satisfy a number of demands. For example, multiple forest management methods can be developed that combine elements of wood production, watershed protection, wildlife and recreation. Agroforestry technologies exist that permit the production of fuelwood or fodder with food crops on the same land, or that combine soil conservation with production.

At the end of Step 4, promising land-use types have been identified and specified in terms of what they have to achieve, for example "integrated arable and livestock farming to increase livestock production and stabilize soil loss". At this stage, however, information about the requirements and potential of these land-use types is very incomplete. Results from Steps 5 and 6 may show that promising options are not viable, thereby making it necessary to reconsider the alternatives in Step 4.

Public and executive discussion of problems and alternatives

A further stage of responsibility now lies with the decision-makers. The planning team prepares the problem statements (from Step 3) and the alternatives for change in terms that are suitable for public and executive discussion: clear, brief summaries, but with detailed evidence available for scrutiny. The alternatives are presented to representatives of the local people, government officials and other interested agencies.

A basic decision is whether, in the light of work to date, the original goals still appear to be attainable. Assuming this to be so, two choices must now be made: which problems are to be given priority and which are the most promising alternatives for further study. Finally, the decision-maker can draw attention to action needed at other levels of land-use planning (e.g. at the national level, arising from a district-level plan) and action desirable outside the scope of land-use planning.

Following these decisions, targets for this subsequent work must be specified. A partial reiteration of Step 2 may now be necessary, planning subsequent steps more specifically than before. If necessary, an additional or revised budget and time schedule must be prepared.

CHECKLIST

Step 4

IDENTIFICATION OF OPPORTUNITIES FOR CHANGE

Responsibility: planning team

❏ Based on the goals from Step 1 and problem statements from Step 3, isolate problems for which solutions other than land-use planning must be sought. Generate a range of options for solving each problem, in terms of:
  – opportunities: the people, land resources, improved technology, economic measures, government action;
  – land-use strategies: no change, maximum production, minimum investment, maximum conservation, maximum equity;
  – kinds of production, the role of conservation, self-reliance versus external investment.

❏ Develop realistic options that best meet the needs of production, conservation and sustainability and that minimize conflicts of land use.

❏ Prepare outline budgets and time frames for each option.

❏ Present the problem statements (from Step 3) and the alternatives for change in terms suitable for public and executive discussion.

Responsibility: decision-makers

❏ Decide if the goals are attainable.

❏ Select the priority problems.

❏ Choose the most promising alternatives for a feasibility study; specify targets.

❏ Specify action needed at other levels of planning.

EVALUATE LAND SUITABILITY

This step forms the central part of *land evaluation*, a procedure which answers the following questions:

- For any specified kind of land use, which areas of land are best suited?
- For any given area of land, for which kind of use is it best suited?

A systematic way of doing this is set out in *A framework for land evaluation* (FAO, 1976) and detailed procedures are given in guidelines on evaluation for rain-fed agriculture, irrigated agriculture, forestry and extensive grazing (see Land evaluation, p.81). In simplified form, the procedure is:

- describe promising *land-use types*;
- for each land-use type, determine the *requirements*, e.g. for water, nutrients, avoidance of erosion;
- conduct the surveys necessary to map *land units* and to describe their physical properties, e.g. climate, slope, soils;
- compare the requirements of the land-use types with the properties of the land units to arrive at a *land suitability classification*.

Land cannot be graded from "best" to "worst" irrespective of the kind of use and management practised because each kind of use has special requirements. For example:

- Rice has high water requirements and most varieties grow best in standing water; no other cereal crop will tolerate waterlogging during its period of active growth.
- Tea, sugar cane and oil-palm need efficient transport to processing plants; most crops grown for subsistence do not.
- For mechanical operations, stones and rock outcrops are limiting; with oxen or hand implements, cultivation can work round these obstacles.

Description of land-use types

A land-use type is a kind of land use described in terms of its products and management practices (Table 3). For reconnaissance surveys at the national level, highly generalized descriptions may be sufficient, e.g. "sorghum production", "conservation forestry". At the district and local levels, it is necessary to specify the use in more detail. For example, will the sorghum production be mechanized or based on animal traction? Will fertilizer be used? Will the conservation forests be managed by the government forestry service or by local communities?

Such descriptions serve two purposes. First, they are the basis for determinating the requirements of a use. Second, the management specifications can be used as a basis for extension services and for planning necessary inputs.

The land-use types will be based on the promising improvements identified in Step 4. They may be modifications of existing uses, such as incorporating fodder trees or soil conservation measures, or something new to the area, such as the introduction of a new cash crop.

Selection of land qualities and land characteristics

Land-use requirements are described by the land qualities needed for sustained production. A *land quality* is a complex attribute of land that has a direct effect on land use. Examples are the availability of water and nutrients, rooting conditions and erosion hazard (Table 4). Most land qualities are determined by the interaction of several *land characteristics*, measurable attributes of the land. For example, the quality "availability of water" is determined by the balance between water demand and water supply. The demand is the potential evaporation from the surface of the crop and the soil; the supply is determined by rainfall, infiltration, storage of water in the soil and the ability of the crop to extract the stored water.

In the case of "availability of water", it is practicable to calculate reliable quantitative values for the land quality. The water demand

TABLE 3
Description of a land-use type

TITLE	Rice cultivation by smallholders
PRODUCTION Marketing arrangements, yields	Grain for subsistence, surplus sold in local market. Straw fed to draught animals. Average yield, 2.6 t/ha. When water is not limited, wet-season yield may be 4 t/ha and dry-season yield may be 5 t/ha
MANAGEMENT UNITS Size, configuration, ownership	Family-owned plots from 0.2 to 2 ha, usually associated with as many as 4 ha of upland which may be up to 2 or 3 km distant
CULTIVATION PRACTICES AND INPUTS Labour, skill, power, varieties, seeds, agrochemicals	**Labour requirements** from 200 person-days/ha without mechanization to 150 person-days/ha where buffaloes or tractors are used. Terraced fields need extra labour to maintain bunds and waterways
	Power requirements. Power for ploughing, harrowing and threshing may be provided by two-wheeled tractors. Alternatively, buffaloes may be used for land preparation or all work may be manual. Tractors may reduce tillage time by 60% and total time between crops by 30%
	Land preparation seeks to control weeds, create a good physical medium for rooting and reduce water seepage loss. This is achieved by ploughing or hoeing twice, followed by harrowing under flooded conditions
	Recommended varieties. Varieties are selected locally to suit specific sites and according to the season. The growing period must be long enough to span the flood period and to allow cultivation and harvesting under favourable conditions.
	Planting rates are 20 to 40 kg/ha, seedlings are spaced from 20x20 to 25x25 cm depending on tillering capacity and length of stalks
	Fertilizer. To replace nutrients removed by a crop of 4 t/ha requires 60 kg N, 30 kg P_2O_5
	Weed control by maintaining adequate water depth and hand weeding until the crop canopy is closed
	Pests and diseases. Chemicals used to control rice blast and stem borers. Good husbandry and resistant varieties control other fungal diseases
CROPPING CHARACTERISTICS	Rice is grown as a monoculture, one or two crops per year. Fallow land is grazed by draught buffaloes and other domestic livestock
WATER	Most crops are rain-fed, with water stored in level, bunded fields. Irrigation, from tanks or by stream diversion, enables a second crop to be grown in the dry season

of a leafy perennial crop, such as sugar cane or rubber, is much greater than that of a crop with a short growing period, for example beans. A soil water storage capacity of 200 mm might be enough in a humid area but not enough where seasonal droughts occur. For major crops, quantitative models have been developed to estimate crop yields under a range of quality values.

In any particular project, only a limited number of land qualities need be selected for use in evaluation. Criteria for selection are:

• The quality must have a substantial effect either on performance or on the costs of production. Some qualities affect most kinds of land use, for example "availability of water"; others are more specific, for example "conditions of ripening" is a quality that affects grain crops but not rubber.

• Critical values of the quality must occur in the planning area. If a quality is adequate everywhere, there is no need to include it. For example, most tropical crops are sensi-

TABLE 4
Land qualities for rain-fed farming

Land qualities	Land characteristics that measure the quality
Availability of energy	Sunshine hours in growing season, temperature regime
Availability of water	Evaporative demand set against rainfall, soil water storage and rooting conditions
Conditions for ripening	Period of successive dry days with specified sunshine and temperature
Climatic hazards	Frequency of damaging frost, hail or winds during growing period
Sufficiency of oxygen in the root zone	Soil drainage class, depth to water-table
Sufficiency of nutrients	Soil nutrient levels, pH, organic matter content
Erosion hazard	Rainfall and wind erosivity set against soil cover, slope angle and length and soil permeability
Toxicity	Levels of soluble Al and Fe; pH

tive to frost but, in most parts of the lowland tropics, the land quality "frost hazard" need not be considered.

Having selected relevant land qualities, it is necessary to decide which land characteristics are to be used for measuring them. For example, the quality "erosion hazard" requires information on rainfall intensity, slope angle and soil properties.

A compromise must be reached between characteristics that most closely define the land quality and those that are less precise but on which information is more readily available. Out of necessity, the choice is limited to those characteristics for which information is already available or can be gathered quickly. If there is no information on a critical land quality, surveys must be carried out or research initiated.

Land evaluations are sometimes conducted directly in terms of land characteristics, e.g. by using rainfall instead of availability of water, slope angle instead of erosion hazard. There is, in fact, a hidden use of land qualities in this way of doing things, since plants do not actually require rainfall but do require water (which might alternatively be obtained from a high water-table in a dry area, for example). In practice, evaluations carried out carefully using either qualities or characteristics give quite similar results.

Mapping of land units and their characteristics

In Step 3, land units were identified as a basis for the diagnosis of problems. It may now be necessary to map these units in more detail, e.g. by dividing land systems into land facets or complex soil mapping units into soil series. The criterion for choice of land units is that they are expected to respond to management in a relatively similar way at the scale of the study.

Whether it is now necessary as part of the land-use plan to conduct original surveys depends on the requirements of the plan and the detail and reliability of the information available. Soil surveys, agroclimatic studies, forest inventories and pasture resource inventories are major sources. For land-use planning at the national level, reconnaissance surveys at scales of about 1:250 000 may be adequate; district-level planning will need at least semi-detailed surveys at a scale of about 1:50 000.

Natural resource surveys take a substantial amount of time and will delay the planning procedure. However, past experience has shown that to proceed with land development projects without adequate resource data can lead to disasters, both for production and conservation. In practice, resource surveys and studies of land-use types can proceed at the same time, with frequent interchanges of information.

TABLE 5
Structure of the FAO land suitability classification

S	SUITABLE	The land can support the land use indefinitely and benefits justify inputs
S1	Highly suitable	Land without significant limitations. Include the best 20-30% of suitable land as S1. This land is not perfect but is the best that can be hoped for
S2	Moderately suitable	Land that is clearly suitable but which has limitations that either reduce productivity or increase the inputs needed to sustain productivity compared with those needed on S1 land
S3	Marginally suitable	Land with limitations so severe that benefits are reduced and/or the inputs needed to sustain production are increased so that this cost is only marginally justified
N	NOT SUITABLE	Land that cannot support the land use on a sustained basis, or land on which benefits do not justify necessary inputs
N1	Currently not suitable	Land with limitations to sustained use that cannot be overcome at a currently acceptable cost
N2	Permanently not suitable	Land with limitations to sustained use that cannot be overcome

Examples of classes in the third category
S2e   Land assessed as S2 on account of limitation of erosion hazard
S2w   Land assessed as S2 on account of inadequate availability of water
N2e   Land assessed as N2 on account of limitation of erosion hazard

Note: There is no standard system for letter designations of limitations; first-letter reminders should be used where possible.

Setting limiting values
for land-use requirements

Limiting values are the values of a land quality or land characteristic that determine the class limits of land suitability for a certain use. The standard FAO land suitability classification is shown in Table 5.

The first and most important decision is to separate land that is suitable from that which is not. Important criteria for deciding on the suitability of land for a specific use are sustainability and ratio of benefits to costs.

- • *The land should be able to support the land use on a sustained basis.* This means that the use must not progressively degrade the land. Many changes of land use cause an initial loss of land resources: for example, when forest is cleared for tea plantations or for arable farming, there is always a loss of forest habitat and wildlife as well as of soil and accumulated plant nutrients.

From then on, a good level of productivity must be maintained by the new system of management. For example, if soil erosion is not controlled, the new land-use type cannot be sustained. According to the land-use type, the upper limit of the land quality "erosion hazard" might be set in terms of slope, as follows:

- – plantation tea, high level of management: 20°
- – smallholder tea, average level of management: 15°
- – rain-fed arable crops with simple soil conservation practices: 8°

- • *The use should yield benefits that justify the inputs.* The user has to make a reasonable living from the land. Local experience will usually be the best guide. Alternatively, a financial analysis can be undertaken.

It is then possible to distinguish up to three classes of suitability, although this is not always necessary. Land classed as highly suitable is the best land for the specified use; moderately suitable land is clearly fit for the use but has limitations; while marginally suitable land

TABLE 6
Example of land requirements for a specified land-use type (bunded rice)

Land qualities	Land characteristics	Limiting values for land characteristics			
		S1	S2	S3	N
Sufficiency of energy	Mean annual temperature, (°C) or	>24	21-24	18-21	<18
	Elevation (m)*	0-600	600-1 200	1 200-1 800	>1 800
Sufficiency of water	75% probability rainfall (mm)	>1 300	900-1 300	500-900	<500
	Soil drainage class	Poorly drained	Imperfectly drained	Moderately well drained	Excessively drained
	Soil texture	C, ZC, ZCL, L	SC, SCL, ZL, Z	SL	S, LS
	Soil depth (cm)	>80	60-80	40-60	<40
Sufficiency of nutrients	pH of flooded soil	6-7	5-6 7-8	4.5-5 8-8.5	<4.5 >8.5
Salinity hazard	EC_e (mS cm^{-1})	<3	3-5	5-7	>7
Ease of water control	Slope angle (degrees)	<1	1-2	2-6	>6
Ease of cultivation	Stones and rock outcrops (%)	Nil	1-5	5-10	>10

* Elevation is used to assess sufficiency of energy where temperature data are not available; these values apply to Sri Lanka.
Source: Dent and Ridgway (1986).

falls near to (but above) the limit for suitability. Land that is not suitable may be subdivided into permanently not suitable, where there are limitations to sustained use that are clearly impractical to overcome; and currently not suitable, where such limitations could be overcome but not at a currently acceptable cost.

The construction of a table of limiting values for each land suitability class (see Table 6) is a central operation in land evaluation. To do this, information is needed on the performance of a land-use type over a range of sites, taken either from trials or the experience of land users.

The land requirements for several individual crops can be combined to assess the needs of a land-use type that includes several crops grown together or in rotation.

Matching land use with land

The first stage in matching is to compare the requirements of each land-use type with the land qualities of each land unit. The simplest procedure is to:

• check measured values of each land quality or characteristic against the class limits;
• allocate each land unit to its land suitability class according to the most severe limitation (Fig. 8).

For cases in which at least one limitation is enough to render the land unsuitable for the use, the method of taking the most severe limitation is valid. For example, for maize cultivation it is of no use having level land and sufficient rainfall if the soils are highly saline. For less severe values of limitations, alternative methods of combining ratings for individual qualities can be used.

Matching, however, can become a wider process than the simple comparison of requirements with qualities. Wherever this initial com-

FIGURE 8
Example of the process of qualitative land suitability classification

Speed of survey	Land characteristics	Start				
Aerial photo interpretation with rapid field surgey	GROUP A	Assume: Class	S1	S2	S3	N
	Slope		✓			
	Past erosion		✓			
	Surface wetness		✓			
	Group A only, S1					
Moderate survey speed A + B	GROUP B					
	Surface stones and rock outcrop		X	✓		
	Unfavourable surface conditions			✓		
	Texture of topsoil			✓		
	Groups A + B, cannot be better than			S2		
Slow survey speed A + B + C	GROUP C					
	Effective soil depth			X	✓	
	Subsoil texture				✓	
	Group A + B + C, cannot be better than				✓	
					S3	

parison shows certain land units to be unsuitable for a given use, the specification of the land-use type can be examined to see if, by modifying it, the suitability of those land units can be raised.

Thus, if suitability has been downgraded owing to erosion hazard, a new land-use type could be designed with the addition of contour-aligned hedgerows or other soil conservation measures. The use of fast-maturing crop varieties in areas with a short growing season is another example. By adapting the land-use types to meet the limitations present in the area in this way, higher overall suitabilities can be achieved.

A further possibility is the introduction of *land improvements,* inputs which bring about relatively permanent improvements in the characteristics of the land. Examples are drainage of land that is too wet or terracing of steeplands. In this way, the land is adapted to the requirements of the land use. Land improvements invariably require maintenance as well as capital expenditure.

Qualitative and quantitative land evaluation
Some decisions need only qualitative land evaluation: for example, identifying the critical importance of certain areas for important land uses such as for an export crop. Quantitative

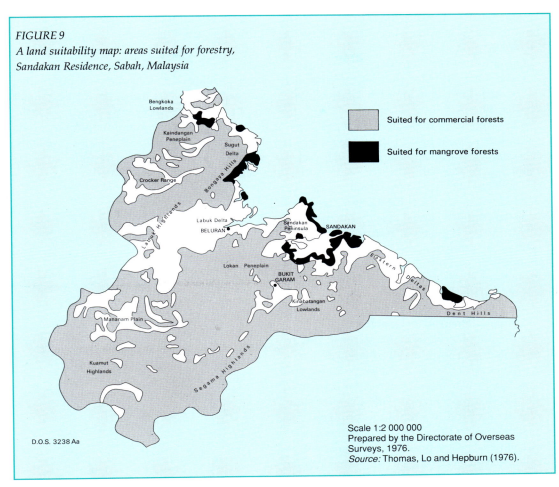

FIGURE 9

A land suitability map: areas suited for forestry,
Sandakan Residence, Sabah, Malaysia

Suited for commercial forests

Suited for mangrove forests

Scale 1:2 000 000
Prepared by the Directorate of Overseas
Surveys, 1976.
Source: Thomas, Lo and Hepburn (1976).

D.O.S. 3238 Aa

economic evaluations, however, require estimates of crop yields, rates of tree growth, or
other measures of performance. It is not realistic
to predict the performance of each land suitability class unless data are available on plant
growth (or other measures of performance) and
the relevant inputs from well-characterized sites,
and unless the physical characteristics of the
land mapping units are equally well known.
Quantitative models have been developed for
several major crops but these demand good
data. Even when predictions are based on carefully controlled trials, they may be confounded
in practice by variations in management. Therefore, try to estimate a range of performance
under the likely standards of management.

Land suitability classification

The comparison of requirements of land-use
types with properties of land units is brought
together in a land suitability classification. Suitability is indicated separately for each land-use
type, showing whether the land is suitable or not
suitable, including – where appropriate – degrees of suitability (Table 5). The major reasons
for lowering the classifications, i.e. the land limitations, should be indicated (because of erosion
hazard in one area or a high water-table in another, for instance). In large or complex surveys
involving many mapping units land evaluation
can be assisted by the use of geographic information systems (see p. 77). A major facility is that, if
the land suitability data are entered into such a

system, when a change is made to one or more limiting values, new maps of land suitability can be rapidly produced.

The outputs from Step 5 are:
- land suitability maps, showing the suitability of each land unit for each land-use type (Fig. 9);
- descriptions of these land-use types.

The descriptions of land-use types are given in a degree of detail appropriate to the level of planning. At the national level, only outline descriptions of major kinds of land use may be needed. At district and local levels, land-use type descriptions should specify the management, inputs (e.g. seeds, fertilizer, fuel) and estimated production (see Table 3). Such information will later be needed to make provision for the supply of inputs and for storage, distribution and marketing (Step 9).

Planning for research

The evaluation process in this step will almost certainly have shown up information deficiencies. The tolerances of plants (or of crop cultivars, tree provenances) to particular land limitations are rarely known with any precision. Where new land-use types are proposed for introduction to the area, it will be necessary to conduct trials (on-station and on-farm) to validate their performance before they can be safely recommended for adoption. Gaps in knowledge of land resources may also have been revealed, thus calling for additional surveys.

It is impracticable to delay the land-use plan until all such research has been completed; but, at the same time, it is unwise to proceed if there is a serious lack of information. Action can be taken in two ways:
- *Outside the land-use plan.* Draw the attention of national and international research agencies as well as universities and donors to the need for research in specified aspects if land development of the area is to proceed on a proper basis of knowledge.
- *Within the land-use plan.* Based on existing local institutions (strengthened if neces-

sary), set up trials or other research activities as part of the land-use plan itself.

Either of these ways will form a "research loop", feeding back information for making more reliable evaluations and more productive and sustainable land use in the future. Do not be put off by the apparently long time scale, three to five years as a minimum, of most kinds of research. By anticipating likely problems, there is a better chance of results becoming available when they are needed.

CHECKLIST

Step 5

LAND SUITABILITY EVALUATION

Responsibility: planning team

❏ Describe land-use types in sufficient detail for subsequent analysis.

❏ Select land qualities and land characteristics to be used in comparisons of land-use requirements with land.

❏ Map the land units and determine their relevant land characteristics and qualities.

❏ Set limiting values to land-use requirements, to be used for determining class limits for land suitability. Take into account sustainability and the ratio of benefits to inputs.

❏ Match land use with land:
  – compare land-use requirements with land qualities or characteristics to determine provisional land suitability classes;
  – consider modifications to land-use types, in order that they become better suited to the land;
  – consider land improvements that could make the land better suited to the land use.

❏ Map land suitability for each land-use type.

❏ Plan for research needed: additional surveys, research by outside agencies or within the land-use plan.

Step 6

APPRAISE THE ALTERNATIVES: ENVIRONMENTAL, ECONOMIC AND SOCIAL ANALYSIS

The evaluation carried out so far has been essentially in terms of physical suitability. An assessment has been made of whether different kinds of land use can be undertaken on a sustained basis.

In Step 6, the effects of each alternative use are appraised in environmental, economic and social terms.

Obviously, these aspects have not been ignored: they generally guided the identification of promising options at Step 4. Now, those that passed this first test are formally appraised against the selected criteria. In this step, it is essential to examine land-use proposals from the standpoint of the capabilities and incentives of individual land users.

Box 8
Measuring the worth of a land-use system

- **Gross margin.** The market value of the produce minus the variable costs that are attributable directly to the product (in the case of an agricultural crop – seeds, fertilizer, fuel, water, labour, hired machinery, etc.).

- **Net margin.** Gross margin minus the fixed costs of production (for example, depreciation of farm equipment, buildings, water distribution, soil conservation works).

- Results of gross margin or net margin analysis can be interpreted in several ways:
  - Which is the best land for each crop or land-use type?
  - Which is the best use for each land unit?
  - Will a proposed change be profitable?

- Partial farm budgeting, calculating only the effects of any proposed changes in land use, is a simple way of projecting the farm-level effects for representative farmers. The difference between net income accruing under a present and an alternative land use is usually referred to as "returns". Investment, maintenance and other costs needed to bring about desired changes in land use are referred to as "costs".

- Where capital investment is involved – for example in land improvements that will lead to a stream of benefits over a long time – discounted cash flow analysis can be used to place the costs and benefits on a comparable basis, i.e. their present value. Money earns interest so its value increases over time. In the same way, income promised in the future is worth less than the same income now, and its present worth can be calculated by the reverse of interest, called discounting. The interest rate assumed for discounting is called the discount rate.

- Discounted cash flow analysis of all benefits and all costs to their equivalent present value produces three measures of the worth of a stream of income which can be used to compare land development options with alternative opportunities for investment:

- **Net present worth.** The present worth of benefits minus present worth of costs.

- **Benefit:cost ratio.** The present worth of benefits divided by the present worth of costs.

- **Internal rate of return.** The rate of discounting at which the present worth of benefits becomes equal to the present worth of costs.

PLATE 5
*Environmental problems from capital works. The Volta Dam, Ghana – Large engineering
projects create dramatic local environmental changes but may also have far-reaching indirect
impacts. A reduction in the sediment load of the Volta River has changed the pattern of coastal
erosion and sedimentation more than 100 km away*

One way of doing this is to model the performance of different options and their effects on representative land users. A word of caution is necessary: quantitative data are not necessarily better, more reliable or more accurate than qualitative data. Sophisticated models need a lot of data and make assumptions that should be clearly understood before the models are applied to particular problems. There will be many cases where a qualitative judgement is more appropriate.

Environmental impact
The land suitability evaluation has already classified as "not suitable" any land use that continually degrades the land. An analysis of environmental impact goes further. It compares what will happen under each alternative system of management in terms of the quality of life of the whole community and takes account of effects both within and beyond (off-site effects) the planning area.

In-depth knowledge of physical, chemical and biological processes and how these interact with society is needed to foresee the likely environmental impact of a specific land-use system. Often, the impact of a particular activity may be long term or several stages removed from the primary cause of the problem. For example, in Sri Lanka coastal erosion and flooding have been caused by the exploitation of protective underwater coral barriers for lime production. In West Africa, current coastal erosion has been attributed to big dams, built on major rivers over 20 years ago, which have intercepted the supply of sediment to the coastal zone (Plate 5).

Following are examples of the environmental effects to be considered:
- *Soil and water resources.* Hazard of soil erosion, landslides and sedimentation; security of water supply and water quality within and beyond the planning area.
- *Pasture and forest resources.* Degradation of rangelands, clearance or degradation of forests.
- *Quality of wildlife habitat.* Structure and composition of forests, grasslands and wetlands; critical areas needed to maintain wild plant and animal communities, including germplasm conservation; side-effects of terrestrial developments on wetland ecosystems;
- *Scenic and recreational value* for tourism and leisure industries. Tolerance of the disturbance associated with leisure, and compatibility with other land uses.

Economic analysis
In Step 5, land suitability is expressed either in qualitative terms (highly, moderately and marginally suitable, or not suitable) or in quantitative physical terms (e.g. crop or timber yield). By comparing the production and other benefits with inputs in terms of money, an extra quantitative measure of land suitability is provided (see Financial and economic analysis, p. 81).

An underlying assumption of financial and economic analysis is that market prices, established in competitive markets, reflect social values. Where there is no competitive market for a resource, which is often the case with renewable land resources and family labour, some other measure of worth has to be found.

Financial analysis looks at profitability from the point of view of a farmer or other private investor, by comparing the producers' revenues with their costs. Farmers will not practise a land use unless, from their point of view, it pays. Financial analysis can answer some immediate, practical questions:
- Is this crop, or land use, the most profitable option?
- Where can this crop be grown, or land use practised, most profitably?

Economic analysis estimates the value of a system of land use to the community as a whole. For example, if prices to the producer are reduced by taxes or held at an artificially high value by subsidies, these taxes or subsidies have to be eliminated to arrive at a *shadow price* for production. Costs have to be treated in the same way.

Where there are clear economic consequences of environmental effects, for example the reduction of sediment in rivers, the money value to the community can be estimated and included in economic analysis.

Comparisons of financial with economic analysis can highlight the need for policy changes. A particular land use, for example high stocking rates on communal grazing land (which is free to the producer), may be degrading pastures and soils, thus destroying land resources. If financial analysis shows the use to be advantageous from the farmers' point of view, it is likely to continue, however environmentally or, in the longer term, socially damaging it is. Economic analysis should take account of damage to land resources and the consequent lowering of their productivity. Policy changes will be needed to make a socially desirable kind of land use equally advantageous to the farmer. Similarly, financial analysis may demonstrate that farmers do not have an incentive to produce a surplus for sale. If government policy requires increased production, a change of pricing policy may be an effective way to provide incentives to achieve the desired change.

Limitations of economic analysis

Economic analysis is easier where there is general agreement on social values and development goals and where there are freely competitive markets. It is complicated where there are distortions of the market or where development brings unintended side-effects, such as pollution or the loss of communal resources, e.g. access to grazing or fuelwood. It is the job of the planner to identify these side-effects and to assess their economic costs.

A serious limitation of economic analysis is that it is biased in favour of quick-yielding investments. The technique of discounted cash flow analysis, which is used to convert costs and benefits arising in the future to present-day values, has the effect that benefits accruing more than about 25 years in the future have virtually no present value at discount rates greater than 10 percent (Figs 10 and 11). This

makes it difficult to justify long-term investments, especially in forestry. The choice of discount rate has more effect on the value of any long-term agricultural or forestry development than the predicted yields of crops or timber.

Finally, costs and prices can change within a few years and projections of their future levels are risky. For example, it may be found that oil-palm is a more profitable crop than rubber at present-day costs and prices but, by the time these crops are producing, the position may have reversed. There is no easy solution to this problem. For perennial crops or forestry, it may prove better to adopt land uses that perform best in physical terms, rather than seeking short-term price advantages. Economic calculations must be updated periodically during the planning period.

Strategic planning

Strategic planning must take a medium- to long-term view to avoid closing options for the future. Land-use policy must take account of land suitability, the current economic situation, the production and services obtainable in relation to the expected future needs and the possibility of meeting demands from elsewhere.

Land with severe physical limitations usually offers few viable options. Land-use planning is more difficult for land that is well suited for many different uses. Besides physical and economic suitability, one needs to know the *critical importance* of land for specified uses. This means estimating not only whether a particular area is physically suitable but also whether it is important that this specific area of land should be used in a particular way. Examples are protected sites for the preservation of rare plant communities or the prevention of urban encroachment on to prime farmland.

This issue can be addressed by first devising realistic alternative scenarios of future needs and then comparing estimates of the potential production with the target production. If a target can be met easily, no particular area of land is likely to be critical for that use and, therefore, flexibility of land use is high. But if most of the

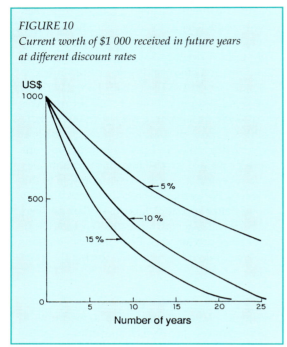

FIGURE 10

*Current worth of $1 000 received in future years
at different discount rates*

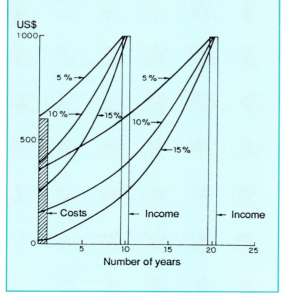

FIGURE 11

*Current worth of a benefit of $1 000 received ten or
20 years hence at different discount rates, compared
with present costs*

physically suitable land will be needed to meet the target, all such land is critical and flexibility of land use is low.

Social impact

The most profitable land use for each parcel of land can be calculated in financial and economic terms but this does not fully represent the effects on the community. Social impact analysis studies the effects of proposed changes on different groups of people. Particular attention should be given to effects on women, ethnic minorities and the poorest sections of the community.

There are no fixed procedures for assessing the social impact of a proposed change of land use. The social purpose of the land-use plan should be laid down at the outset and the impact of each system of land use can be judged against this goal. Examples of social factors that might be considered are:

- *Population.* Its projected size, distribution and age structure; the desirability or otherwise of migration.
- *Basic needs.* Food security, lessening of risk (e.g. in planning subsistence production as compared with cash cropping).
- *Employment and income opportunities.* For example, mechanization may have been considered as a means of achieving lower production costs but this could lead to unemployment.
- *Land tenure and customary rights.* For example, grazing and water rights.
- *Administrative structure and legislation* within which planning must operate.
- *Community stability.*

Understanding how present land-use decisions are made is essential in order to understand the full economic and social implications of any proposed change. *Farming systems analysis* can provide an integrated view by taking the farm family as the decision-making unit. The case will often be that, what appears to be the optimum land use when viewed from a district level, is impracticable at the farming system level. This is because individual families have to satisfy their needs from their own farm, which will not include all kinds of land nor the same proportions as the district or catchment as a whole.

Interface of land-use planning with rural development planning

Often, a change in land use will require investment in physical infrastructure (roads, storage and processing facilities) and services (market-ing, credit, veterinary). New or enlarged settlements also need infrastructure and social services, such as water supply, health and education services. These social gains from a rural development plan may compensate for benefits that have to be foregone, such as the restriction of communal grazing. In this respect, land-use planning merges with rural development planning while changes in land use may support improved facilities for the community.

CHECKLIST

Step 6

APPRAISAL OF ALTERNATIVES:
ENVIRONMENTAL, ECONOMIC AND SOCIAL ANALYSIS

Responsibility: planning team

❏ The following studies refer first to individual combinations of land use with land units that have been classed as suitable in physical terms and, second, to alternative combinations of land use that are being considered in the plan.

– *Environmental impact assessment:* soil and water resources, pasture and forest resources, wildlife conservation, resources for tourism and recreation; off-site effects.

– *Financial analysis:* are the proposed land-use types profitable for the farmer or other land users?

– *Economic analysis:* what is the value of the proposed changes to the community, within and beyond the planning area?
Are there areas of land of critical importance (for production or conservation) for certain uses?

– *Social impact:* what effects will the proposed changes have on different sections of the community, especially women, minority groups and the poor?

– *Strategic planning:* how do the proposed changes in land use affect wider aspects of rural development planning, including national goals?

CHOOSE THE BEST OPTION

Planning as a decision support system

At the point of decision, the roles of the planner and the decision-maker must interact. The planner has to assemble and summarize the facts needed to make an informed decision – namely the results obtained from the previous steps. The decision-maker has to choose the land-use option that best meets the goals.

Figure 12 represents decision-making as a process of choosing between a range of options, with the preceding steps of land-use planning shown as a decision support system. It may be obvious which option is best, or else the choice may involve careful judgement.

In simple cases, a good decision may be made by intuitively weighing the evidence that has been built up through the previous steps of planning.

Land-use allocation, recommendation and assistance

In the simplest planning situation, that of new land settlement, land units can be allocated to specific uses. Settlers are then brought in and, at least initially, required to practise those uses.

Far more commonly nowadays, the land is already settled and is being cultivated, grazed, etc., so the purpose of the plan is to help solve problems of existing land-use systems. In this situation, land use cannot be simply "allocated". New land-use types can be recommended for specific areas, through extension services and through provision of inputs and services.

Decisions on land allocation or land-use recommendation for competing uses begin with:

- a set of *policy guidelines*, for example – a minimum acceptable production of staple foods and fuelwood, the preferred location

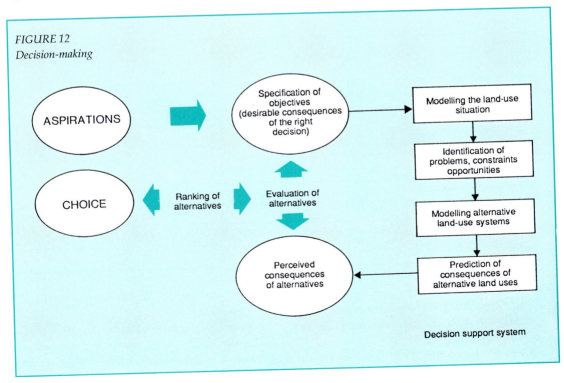

FIGURE 12
Decision-making

ASPIRATIONS

Specification of objectives (desirable consequences of the right decision)

Modelling the land-use situation

Identification of problems, constraints opportunities

CHOICE

Ranking of alternatives

Evaluation of alternatives

Modelling alternative land-use systems

Perceived consequences of alternatives

Prediction of consequences of alternative land uses

Decision support system

TABLE 7

Example of a goals achievement matrix: Dedza District, Malawi

	1. Data from Step 6			
Land-use type	Net income (#) per ha	Net income (#) per caput	Population carrying capacity per km²	Environmental impact
Annual crops with livestock, improved management, 1.6 ha farms	113	36	312	Moderate
Annual crops without livestock, improved management, 3 ha farms	50	30	167	Moderate
Coffee, improved management, 1.6 ha farms	-10	-16	156	Low
Ranching	-2	75	3	Low
Forestry	63	51	63	Low

	2. Goals achievement, as a percentage of the best option for each criterion			
Land-use type	Return per ha	Return per caput employed	Population carrying capacity	Environmental impact
Annual crops with livestock	100	48	100	70
Annual crops only	44	40	54	60
Ranching	2	100	1	90
Forestry	56	68	40	100

	3. Goals achievement, weighted by the decision-maker's judgement of the importance of each criterion				
Land-use type	Return per ha	Return per caput	Population carrying capacity	Environmental impact	Total goals achievement
Weighting	**0.3**	**0.2**	**0.3**	**0.2**	**1.0**
Annual crops with livestock	30	10	30	14	84
Annual crops only	13	8	16	12	49
Ranching	1	20	1	18	39
Forestry	17	14	12	20	63

Source: Dent and Young (1981).

within range of existing services and a limited amount of development capital;
• *land units,* delineated by a natural resource survey;
• *land-use types,* designed to be sustainable

and economically viable within the planning area.

Sometimes it is helpful to set out the options in a goals achievement matrix and rank them according to the chosen criteria. Table 7 gives

TABLE 8
Example of a summary table of land use: Walapane AGA, Sri Lanka

Land use by crop	Potential area	Area actually used	Areas planned for change this year	Estimated production this year
		(hectares)		*(tonnes)*
Irrigable land				
Double cropped rice	1 840	650	+140	1 500
Single cropped rice	–	450	-32	800
Rain-fed arable land				
Bunded rice	2 250	1 610	-108	1 750
Tobacco	–	1 900	-300	...
Subsistence upland crops	<4 000	2 000	-200	...
Other chena land	–	2 320	-100	...
Improved mixed cropping + livestock	–	48	+200	140 l.u.
Tea				
Estate seedling	–	6 500	-120	3 900
Clonal	5 250	370	+120	250
Smallholders	–	120	No change	48
Forest				
Dense	29 980	1 630	No change	Reserve
Open	–	3 110	No change	...
Scrub	–	1 190	-280	...
Plantation	–	4 780	+400	4 000 m³
Grassland	Not estimated	1 070	No change	400 l.u.
Urban	Not estimated	10	No change	–
Water	490	490	No change	–
Unusable land	130	130	No change	–

Note:
... data not available.
l.u. = livestock units.

an example. First, the predicted performance of several promising land-use types is set out according to four criteria. Next, the options are rated according to how well they satisfy each criterion. Finally, weightings are allotted to each criterion, reflecting the decision-maker's judgement of the extent to which it should influence land use. No one is likely to make a decision solely on the "percentage goals achievement", but this procedure draws attention to the subjective weightings that are being used and the less beneficial as well as the favourable consequences of a particular decision.

The tasks of storage, retrieval and interpretation of a large and heterogeneous mass of information can be assisted by computerized methods. These can can be used for the repetitive

task of comparing the predicted performance of land units against multiple criteria and can present the user with the consequences of alternative decisions in terms of the optimum land-use pattern and goals achievement.

For the increasingly complex tasks of selecting sites for development projects, allocating land among several land uses, developing policies on land use as well as allocating resources, hundreds of individual land units and many alternative land uses may have to be considered. The decision-maker must take into account a variety of practical considerations, including:

- the expressed preferences of the local people;
- the interests of minority groups;

TABLE 9
Example of a tabular plan format[1]

Land units	Mountains	Basins		
	12-28° slopes	Terrace	Bottomland	Steep knolls
				8-20° slopes
Present land use	Subtropical mixed broadleaf forest, 30% degraded	Well-managed paddy, tobacco and vegetables		Badly managed tea or waste
Problems	Accessibility, landslips, soil erosion on recently logged sites	Water shortage in dry periods; low incomes, modest rice yield on coarser soils. Flooding in bottomland. Water pollution from paper mill effluent		Severe soil erosion; low yields
Planned changes	Replant degraded land. Bamboo and spruce plantations on lower gentle slopes; pines on poorer sites	Increased fertilizer use and high-yielding rice on best paddy soils to release more permeable soils for irrigated fruit-trees	Fish pond project	Upgrade better tea sites. Farm woodlots of quick-growing species for the rest
Standards	Strict control of logging within limits of regeneration. Extraction routes to avoid landslip hazards	Upgrade extension services. Advise on agrochemical practices to avoid pollution. Weirs to control water supply. Do not use field runoff for fish ponds. Divert paper mill effluent		For tea, mulch during replanting and pruning; build back-sloping terraces and protected waterways

[1] This is essentially a legend to the planning map which shows the land units and locations of special projects such as the fish ponds and farm woodland projects.

- national policies;
- constraints, e.g. of land tenure and availability of inputs;
- the maintenance of environmental standards;
- practicability – potential implementing agencies should be consulted;
- costs and the availability of funding.

At this point the decision-maker can appraise the overall situation and, if dissatisfied with the achievement of any particular policy guideline, can adjust the weighting of the criteria or introduce new ones. With the aid of a computer, a new land-use pattern and its suitability scores can be produced quickly and, perhaps over several iterations between the decision-maker and the decision support system, an optimum solution may be arrived at.

Good land-use decisions can be arrived at without the assistance of a computerized decision support system. The procedure is the same whether a computer is used or not but the computer package enables the decision-maker to take account of much more information and to learn from predicted consequences of alternative decisions.

Second major consultation
The draft plan should now be submitted for public scrutiny. This is the last chance to bring in outside opinions about the plan and, for most people, it is their first chance to find out in detail what the plan is supposed to achieve and how it will affect them.

In the final analysis, most land-use decisions will be taken by the thousands of individual land users, all making decisions from their own points of view. Use every available means to achieve public involvement – through meetings, posters, the press, broadcasts and government agencies. Many countries have no established tradition or mechanism for public consultation. Consultation may be organized through government, political party mechanisms or traditional systems.

Allow adequate time for reviews and comments, as determined by the decision-maker or planning regulations, and fix a deadline for the receipt of comments.

Review comments and resolve conflicts

Since the comments may be numerous, a systematic process for dealing with them must be adopted. The planners can:

- group the comments according to land use, land users or products;
- assign comments by subject area to a member of the planning team for responses;
- list proposed changes in the draft plan;
- submit comments, responses and proposed changes to the decision-maker.

The decision-makers must decide:

- whether the responses to the comments are adequate;
- which, if any, changes should be made to the draft plan.

Not everyone will be satisfied with the plan. Whatever compromises or adjustments are made, there will still be people who disagree. This should not prevent most of the community from benefiting from the plan. Some way must be found to resolve conflicts. Essentially, this has to be by negotiation, with all sides having the opportunity to prepare and present their case. The consequences of decisions at different planning levels, above and below that of the plan, must be considered, with two-way flows of information (see Fig. 1).

The critical point in Step 7 is reached with selection of the option that is judged to be the best. This forms the basis for subsequent preparation of the plan. The data and evaluation of other options are not discarded, but recorded in the report, since they may be needed for later revision.

Finally, the decision-maker must authorize subsequent steps; that is, the preparation of the chosen plan. At the local level, this may simply require an executive decision, with preparation and implementation proceeding directly. At the district level, there may now be a need to formulate implementation as a new project re-quiring further funding and additional staff, in which case there will be a time delay between Steps 7 and 8. At the national level, the most likely action at this point is for the "national master land-use plan" (or similar title) to be submitted for approval at the highest level of government, after which it will form the basis for policy decisions.

CHECKLIST

Step 7

CHOICE OF THE BEST OPTION

Responsibility: planning team

❑ Set out a series of options for the allocation or recommendation of land-use types to land units. Also state their evaluation in terms of land suitability and environmental, economic and social analysis.

❑ Set out the consequences of these options in terms of the goals and planning objectives.

❑ Present the options and their consequences in a way that is appropriate for review.

Responsibility: planning team and decision-makers

❑ Make arrangements for consultations with the communities affected as well as with the implementing agencies; obtain views about feasibility and acceptability.

❑ Assemble and review the comments received. In the light of these, make any necessary changes to the options.

Responsibility: decision-makers

❑ Decide if the response to comments is adequate.

❑ Consider the options in terms of goals and policy criteria.

❑ Choose the best option.

❑ Authorize preparation of the plan.

PREPARE THE LAND-USE PLAN

At this point, a report is written which has two major functions:
- to present the plan that is now recommended, with reasons for the decisions taken – that is, to summarize the results from Steps 1 to 7;
- to prepare for implementation.

The preferred option for change must be put into a form in which it can be reviewed and, when approved, acted on. A specific land-use plan, intended to be implemented as a development project, is the principal way of doing this. However, depending on the level and purposes of the planning study, the results may also be implemented as guidelines for priorities or by being incorporated into legislation, development budgets, agency programmes, management standards and extension programmes.

The following discussion relates mainly to results being incorporated into a specific land-use plan that is implemented as a development project.

Three elements in the plan that is now prepared are:
- What should be done? – the selected changes to land use and where they should be applied or recommended.
- How should it be done? – logistics, costs and timing.
- Reasons for the decisions taken.

Preparation of maps

Land-use planning is critically concerned with what should be done, where. The planning procedure so far has been based on the fact that land conditions are highly variable and so land-use types that will be sustainable and economically viable on one land unit will fail, in either or both of these respects, on other kinds of land. Hence, maps form a key element in the presentation of results.

Several sets of maps have been prepared as part of the planning procedure: base maps, summaries of available data and possibly maps based on original surveys (Steps 3 and 5); land suitability maps (Step 5); and allocations or recommendations of land use to areas of land (Step 7). These are now drawn up and printed so that they can be used as a basis for implementation and revision.

These maps will be used in the field and in the office by a variety of people – executive, technical and administrative. For the maps to be useful, the following points should be observed:
- The base-map detail (roads, tracks, settlements, administrative boundaries) should be clear; users will constantly need to find where they are and what should be done, where.
- At the same time, the features shown in the maps (e.g. land-use types, soils, water resources) should be easy to see; a good quality of cartography, normally using colour, is essential.
- The legend (key) must be an integral part of the maps.
- The maps should be printed in sufficient quantities to supply all implementing agencies with copies for several years.

Maps are in no way a supplementary part of the report. On the contrary, it may be nearer the truth to say that the text supplements the maps, although they in fact complement each other. The map showing land-use allocations and recommendations is the focal point of the land-use plan.

Writing the plan

The first need is to set out, in summary form and then in more detail, the land-use allocations or recommendations that were selected in Step 7. In this initial presentation, under a heading such as "Land-use recommendations", set out the selected option, without confusing the reader by references to rejected alternatives. This part of the text will be read by those who

FIGURE 13
Mapping development possibilities (Kaduna Plains, Nigeria)

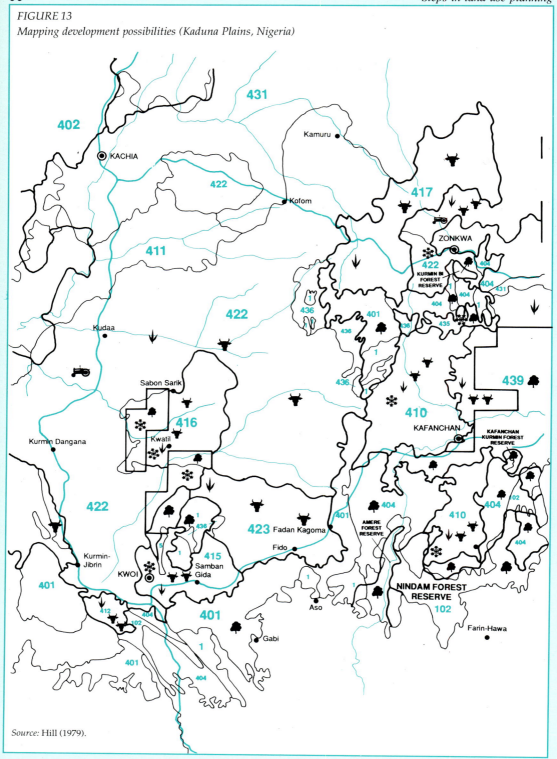

Source: Hill (1979).

Type of development		Summary definition of development
1. Integrated agriculture	(a) In densely cultivated areas	Establishment of integrated agricultural development projects aimed at increasing existing agricultural production per hectare by improving infrastructure (communications, supply of agricultural inputs, produce marketing, credit facilities and extension service coverage). Run by a semi-autonomous project authority, making use of self-help wherever possible. Allied to general improvement of social services.
	(b) In sparsely cultivated areas	As above but also able to increase production by increasing the area under cultivation and/or introducing "mixed farming".
2. Mechanized farming		Establishment of large mechanized farms (>1 000 ha), requiring a high level of management expertise and mechanization of all stages of production from land preparation to harvest. Good planning and adequate conservation measures are essential. Limited to sparsely cultivated areas.
3. Traditional grazing		Improvement of traditional grazing, including control of stock numbers, the elimination of unregulated burning and the introduction of forage species into natural grassland. These measures, together with the establishment of grazing reserves and the allocation of grazing rights, are components of a suggested programme to be organized at the interstate level. Limited to sparsely cultivated areas.
4. Grazing reserves		Establishment of reserves in the major traditional wet- and dry-season grazing areas and along migration routes, with additional reserves within areas freed or being freed by the tsetse eradication programme. Provision of adequate water supplies, veterinary services and improved natural grassland coupled with strict control of stock numbers. Limited to sparsely cultivated areas.
5. Cattle ranches and dairy farming		Establishment of ranches for "growing out" cattle drawn from Fulani herds. Stock numbers restricted to 2 000 head until the viability of the ranch is established. Area not less than 2 000 ha per 1 000 head of cattle with 1 200 ha for wet-season and early dry-season grazing and 800 ha for fodder grass to provide additional dry-season roughage. Supplementary dry season feeding by cottonseed, cottonseed cake, groundnut cake, brewer's grains or molasses as available. Limited to sparsely cultivated areas. Establishment of dairy herds of not more than 100 milking cows. Total area not less than 250 ha with 130 ha improved pastures for wet- and early dry-season grazing and 50 ha to provide additional dry-season feed, supplemented by locally available concentrates and crop residues.
6/7. Production forestry	**6.** Development for production of **timber**	Development financed and managed by government and covering a few to 100 ha in one location, usually for sawn timber production for local use. Alternatively, run by a commercial company at a minimum annual planting rate of 400 ha for sawn timber or pulp. Confined to forest reserves.
	7. Development for production of **fuelwood and poles**	(a) Production by state and federal departments in forest reserves.
		(b) Production by farmers on small woodlots, backed by extension service.
		(c) Extraction from areas of natural vegetation in forest reserves.
8. Protection forestry: reservation to protect areas against erosion or strict conservation measures		Protection of existing and establishment of new forest reserves in areas with slopes greater than 10% (6°) where conservation is required.
		Protection required only in parts of the area.

need to know what is to be done next. An important part is a description of the selected land-use types, including their management specifications and the land units for which they are recommended.

Following this, reasons for the choices and decisions made must be given, again both in outline and in some detail. These explanations are needed by funding agencies wishing to review the soundness of the proposals from technical, economic or other viewpoints. The basic data also constitute a baseline for future monitoring and revision of the plan. The more basic information available, the easier it becomes to revise the plan in the future (Step 10).

Logistic planning

The planner must next consider the practical details of implementing the plan: decide the means, assign responsibility for getting the job done and lay down a timetable for implementation. Set targets that are realistically obtainable, not based on optimism. It may be possible to use experience from previous development programmes to indicate the rate of change that can be achieved in practice. Certainly, the plan must be in accordance with what the people concerned are prepared to do.

Logistic planning is a wide-ranging process, calling for previous experience of similar projects. Some guidelines for tasks that need to be done are:

- Draw up a planning base map, showing areas chosen for development year by year. Tabulate these areas.
- Based on the above, itemize the needs for:
  - land improvements;
  - supporting services;
  - physical infrastructure;
  - credit and other internal financial services.
- On the same basis, together with the management specifications for land-use types, calculate the inputs needed, for example:
  - seed/germplasm (crop cultivars, tree provenances);
  - fertilizers, by type;
  - pesticides;

- irrigation equipment.
- Plan priority land improvements, for example water storage and supply, roads, drains and other engineering works.
- Plan extension programmes and incentives.
- Identify who is to be responsible for which activity. In particular, junior staff must know what is expected of them and must be given adequate incentives.
- Ensure that there are adequate arrangements for financing staff costs, inputs and credit.
- Give particular attention to provision for maintenance of all capital works.
- Discuss the details of the arrangements with the decision-maker and relevant agency staff in terms of:
  - feasibility and acceptability;
  - availability of advisory staff;
  - availability of logistic support;
  - availability of supervision.
- Assess the need for staff training.
- Make the necessary arrangements for research, within the plan or through outside agencies.
- Establish a procedure for reviewing the plan's progress (Step 10).

Staffing, timing and costs

As one form of summary of the logistic planning, list the requirements for implementation in terms of:

- Staffing: specialists, technical staff, labour.
- Timing: the intended scheduling of changes, drawn up as tables.
- Costs: the finance needed to implement the plan, its scheduling year by year and proposed sources of funding.
- Financial control, including independent audit.

Format of the plan

One of the main difficulties in drafting a land-use plan is the wide range of readership that needs to be informed. This ranges from senior government ministers, who have time only to read outline summaries of what is to be done, to technical staff responsible for implementation and the field extension staff who will have to apply the findings to local areas.

To meet the needs of these different users, it has frequently been found useful to divide the plan into the following sections:

- *Executive summary.* Written for non-technical decision-makers; a summary of the land-use situation, its problems, the opportunities and the recommendations for action, i.e. the focal point. Reasons for decisions taken are given, but only briefly. Clear, concise writing is of the highest importance. This section should include at least one key map, the (master) land-use plan and possi-

bly other maps at small scales. It is typically 20 to 50 pages long at the most.

- *Main report.* Explains the methods, findings and factual basis of the plan. Written for technical and planning staff who want to know details, including reasons for decisions taken. Often five to ten times as long as the executive summary.
- *Maps volume.* An integral part of the main report, presented separately for convenience of binding.
- *Appendixes.* Give the technical data that support the main report. These may run to several volumes. They include the results from original surveys conducted as part of

---

Box 9
Example of headings for a land-use plan

TITLE

Land-use plan for ...

- Note that until the plan has been approved by the decision-maker, it is a "proposed land-use plan".

SUMMARY

- Highlight problems, recommendations and the main reasons for these recommendations.

INTRODUCTION

- The long-term goals for the planning area and the purpose of the plan.
- Relationship with other documents. Briefly describe legislation and any higher-level plans as well as local plans that are related to this plan.
- Description of the planning area. A brief overview of location, area, population, land resources, current land use and production.

MANAGEMENT PROBLEMS AND OPPORTUNITIES

- Statement of land-use problems and opportunities.
- Rationale for the selected option.
- Summary of the changes the plan will bring about, by subject area or geographic area.

DIRECTION

- List land-use types and standards that apply to the whole planning area and to individual planning units.
- Identify projects. Illustrate with maps and diagrams.
- Time scale for action.

MONITORING AND REVISION

- Describe the procedure for reviewing progress and revising the plan.

WORK PLAN FOR IMPLEMENTATION

- List individual projects with details of location, time, resources required and responsibility for implementation.

APPENDIXES

- Supporting information:
  - physical environment, planning units, agroclimate and soil data;
  - population, settlement, infrastructure, tenure;
  - present land use;
  - land-use types and land requirements;
  - land suitability;
  - economic projections.

the plan, e.g. soil surveys, forest inventories, records of river flow.

Public relations material

Relatively few people will read the full planning document, a larger number will read the executive summary, but a lot of people need to be informed about the plan. Each implementing agency needs clear instructions, set in the context of the plan as a whole.

Equally important is a range of public information documents, posters and press releases which are needed to inform the people about the plan, its relevance, the benefits to the community as a whole and the participation needed from different sections of the community. This additional material will draw on the main report but should be specially prepared and well illustrated to secure the most effective participation of all parties.

CHECKLIST

Step 8

PREPARATION OF THE PLAN

Responsibility: planning team

❏ Prepare maps – the basic or master land-use plan and supporting maps.

❏ Set out the land-use allocations and recommendations, based on the preferred option selected in Step 7. Give descriptions of land-use types, including management recommendations on each kind of land.

❏ Set targets for achievement, by land-use type, area and agency. Specify how they will be reached. Check that they are within the capabilities of the agencies and infrastructure.

❏ Draw up logistic preparations, specifying the capital works, recurrent inputs and responsibilities for implementation.

❏ Establish mechanisms for monitoring progress and revising the plan (Step 10).

❏ Make arrangements for research needed to support the plan.

❏ Determine the finance needed for each operation and determine sources of funds.

❏ Write the report – executive summary, main report, maps and appendixes.

❏ Establish mechanisms for communication with, and the participation of, all institutions involved.

❏ Prepare public relations material.

Step 9

IMPLEMENT THE PLAN

The objective of the entire land-use planning exercise so far has been to identify and put into practice beneficial land-use changes. Hence, implementation is included as a "step" in the planning process, albeit a step of a different nature.

At the national level, implementation is likely to be through policy guidelines which may also serve as a framework for selection of possible projects at the district level. In this sense, the planning team remains throughout a part of implementation, supplying information to government as a basis for decisions.

At the local level, implementation is sometimes carried out almost contemporaneously with planning. The planning team may move from one locality to another and draw up detailed plans for implementation (within a framework set at the district level), while leaving the local extension staff, village agricultural committees or other local agencies to put the plan into practice. At the district level, the plan will frequently be implemented by means of a development project. There may be a time gap between planning and implementation for financial, bureaucratic or political reasons. The responsibility for putting the plan into effect rests with the decision-makers, the implementing agencies and the people of the area.

The decision-makers have to release funds, instruct sectoral agencies and facilitate the work of private-sector collaborators. Governments may use incentives such as grants and subsidies and may introduce regulations. Sectoral agencies such as the Forestry, Agriculture and Irrigation Departments may work directly where they have the necessary staff and experience; alternatively, they may work indirectly by training as well as through extension services, field demonstrations and workshops.

The role of the planning team

The planning team has several important contributions to make to implementation. The first is simply to ensure that the measures recommended in the plan are correctly understood and put into practice by the implementing agencies. Representatives of the planning team form an essential link between planning and implementation.

Related to this, the planning team can take a lead in coordinating the activities of the implementing agencies and generally maintain communications between all parties to the plan. It can assist in institution-building, the strengthening of existing institutions or, where necessary, the formation of new ones. This can include staff education and training.

A further activity regards public relations. This may include explaining the land-use situation and plan to the media, at public meetings and in schools. The planning team is in a particularly good position to organize research related to the plan, since they are aware of the problems likely to be encountered. Finally, the team will monitor and evaluate the success of the plan (Step 10).

Much time may be needed to ensure the comprehension, participation and satisfaction of the people of the area as well as that of the local and national government authorities. This is clear in the case of the more socially oriented activities such as pasture management committees, cooperatives and credit for small farmers, yet it applies at all levels. Public relations should not be a one-way process of government "explaining" actions to the people, but a two-way interchange of ideas. If members of the local community say, for example, that it would be unwise to graze cattle in a particular area during the dry season, they may have excellent reasons which the implementation team should take into account.

Implementation will often depend on efficient project management. The time, finance and other resources devoted to it will often considerably exceed those of the entire plan-

PLATE 6
Discussion and coordination is essential at many levels

ning process preceding it. Implementation involves many aspects that lie beyond the scope of these guidelines, hence the brevity of this section.

Two aspects which lie at the interface between planning and implementation will be noted: they are institution-building and participation.

Institution-building

It has never been established that the efficient use of land depends on long-term planning. For one thing, the means of implementing long-term plans to date have not proved very effective. Indeed, many government attempts to make farmers conform with (misguided) land-use plans can now be seen as counterproductive.

An opposing view is that land use is best left to market forces, i.e. to a large number of decisions taken by individuals for their own private ends. By keeping decisions small, there is time to learn from both successes and failures, and economic forces will encourage land users to make the best use of resources. This argument rests on decisions being taken where the information is complete but, in fact, individual land users are not always well aware of the consequences of their actions. Without government support, many options are not open to them. Economic pressures can force land users into actions to supply their short-term needs, which will have adverse consequences in the future.

Whatever degree of public intervention is chosen, a professional team is needed to build up an informed opinion on the management of the land and to advise decision-makers on the range of options open and the consequences of alternative decisions. This team needs both the support of the people on the ground and the authority and resources of government.

Government agencies and budgets are mainly organized by sector (Agriculture, Livestock, Forestry, Irrigation Departments, etc.). Land-use planning has to cut across these administrative hierarchies; however, it must do this without appearing to challenge the influence and budget of established institutions.

Attempts at integrated planning are commonly frustrated by:

- ill-defined responsibilities for coordination of sectoral activities and regional administrations;
- inadequate cooperation with national and regional authorities and with specialist agencies, leading to inefficient use of the available data and expertise;
- lack of experienced staff and the absence of a career structure.

Bureaucratic conflicts can be avoided by hiring consultants to prepare a plan, but experience suggests that plans commissioned from consultants are not often used unless external funding has been built in. Typically, there is little local involvement and neither the executive nor the sectoral agencies have the commitment to implement them. There are two proven alternative strategies:

- *Set up a special planning area* with its own budget and administration (e.g. the Tennessee Valley Authority). This avoids interagency conflicts by replacing the existing agencies, but it is costly and takes time.
- *Set up an independent land-use planning unit* (Fig. 14). This will need a range of expertise, access to authority and the ability to make quick decisions. If it is yet another sectoral body, it will merely compete with other agencies and will not be in a strong position either to influence their programmes or to implement plans of its own.

Probably, the most effective role for the land-use planning unit is as a direct support to the executive. At the highest level, land-use planning might be dealt with by a small committee of permanent members drawn from appropriate departments or agencies with a technical (rather than administrative) secretary. The land-use planning committee should make recommendations on priorities, the allocation of resources and the establishment, approval and coordination of land development programmes. Above all, the chain of responsibility must be clear.

At the national level, the committee will need the professional support of a land-use planning

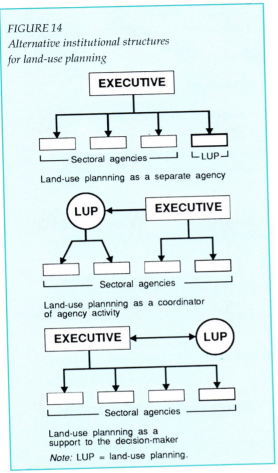

FIGURE 14
Alternative institutional structures
for land-use planning

EXECUTIVE

Sectoral agencies   ⌐LUP⌐

Land-use plannning as a separate agency

LUP   EXECUTIVE

Sectoral agencies

Land-use plannning as a coordinator
of agency activity

EXECUTIVE   LUP

Sectoral agencies

Land-use plannning as a
support to the decision-maker

Note: LUP = land-use planning.

Among the many reasons for this are:
- that the right questions be addressed – different groups of people can have very different perceptions of land-use problems and opportunities, and specialists do not always know best;
- to make use of the fund of local knowledge of the land and the economy of its use;
- to draw on the inventiveness of local people, technical staff and administrators – locally developed solutions will be accepted and implemented more quickly than external technology;
- planning time and skills are limited, so planning down to the last detail is not a realistic option – if land users are committed to the broad outlines of the plan, they will attend to the details anyway.

The planners must work to secure the commitment of all parties to whatever consensus is arrived at in the land-use plan. The surest way of achieving this is to keep all parties informed at every stage of the process, and to make use of the skills and knowledge that they have to offer. If there are no procedures for consultation, then these must be devised and put into effect.

Participation is of the highest importance in incremental planning. This involves building up and documenting knowledge of the land-use situation and identifying important gaps in that knowledge. On the one hand, it requires strengthening the capacities of local communities and decision-makers to make use of the planners' information. On the other, it involves helping decision-makers to focus on land-use goals, the underlying causes of problems and the range of opportunities open to them.

unit responsible for technical aspects of planning, a national land resources database, training and backup for district-level planners. At the district level, staff needs will be more modest, perhaps just one district land-use planner will be required to coordinate district sectoral agencies. Again, the planner should be directly responsible to the chief executive officer and not to a particular department.

Participation

It should be clear from all that has been said that land-use planning must involve the local community, the technical agencies and decision-makers at all levels. Their participation has to be built into the planning process.

CHECKLIST

Step 9

IMPLEMENTATION OF THE PLAN

Responsibility: implementing agencies and planning team together

Implementation involves a wide range of practical activities, many of which lie beyond the scope of these guidelines. The following refer specifically to roles that the planning team may undertake.

❏ Ensure that the changes recommended in the plan are correctly applied in the plan; be available for technical consultations; discuss with implementing agencies any suggested modifications.

❏ Help to maintain communications between all people and institutions participating in or affected by the plan, i.e. land users, sectoral agencies, government, non-governmental organizations, commercial organizations.

❏ Assist in coordination of the activities of the implementing agencies.

❏ Assist in institution-building by strengthening links between existing institutions, forming new bodies where necessary and strengthening cooperation.

❏ Focus on the participation of the land users; ensure adequate incentives.

❏ Organize research in association with the plan; ensure that results from research are communicated and, where appropriate, incorporated into the plan.

❏ Arrange for education and training of project staff and land users.

MONITOR AND REVISE THE PLAN

Now the planning process comes full circle. Information is needed on how well the plan is being implemented and whether it is succeeding, so that the implementation agencies can improve the way in which the plan is being applied and so that the planning team may learn from experience and respond to changing conditions. It is necessary to know:

- Are the land-use activities being carried out as planned?
- Are the effects as predicted?
- Are the costs as predicted?
- Have the assumptions on which the plan was based proved to be correct?
- Are the goals still valid?
- How far are the goals being achieved?

Monitoring

Data are needed to answer all these questions, but data collection must not be allowed to become an end in itself. The more time spent gathering data, the less available for analysis and action. Focus on readily measurable outputs or land conditions relevant to the planning goals and use established methods of data collection such as product sales records. Rank the importance of items to be measured, so that time and budget constraints do not prevent important data from being acquired. Crop yield, rates of tree growth and livestock production are obvious indicators. Other critical data sets are linked to the nature of the plan; for example, the monitoring of water availability in irrigation projects or of river sediment load in projects intended to check erosion.

Monitoring may involve observations at key sites, regular extension visits and discussions with officials and land users. A checklist and periodic meetings in the planning area may serve the purpose. Those responsible for plan implementation should list the tasks needed to correct problems as they arise and should also take action.

Review and revision

By analysis of the data collected, compare what has been achieved with what was intended. Identify problems in the implementation of the plan, or in the data or assumptions on which the plan is based.

There are a wide variety of reasons for failure. The first is that the plan was found to be based on incorrect assumptions; for example, that low crop yields were caused by a lack of fertilizer when in fact the major constraint is water. There may be changes in economic circumstances, such as when the world price of a cash crop falls. Often, failures occur in the logistics of implementation; if monitoring finds that fertilizers are not reaching farmers, is this a result of inefficiencies in the distribution system? Lastly, there may be problems of communication and participation, such as farmers who are not in fact planting the multipurpose trees that are recommended. Such problems should first be approached by finding out the reasons through talking to farmers.

Try to find solutions to the problems and discuss them with those who have to initiate corrective action. For minor changes, this can be at the level of the implementing agencies, for example in the form of revised extension advice. More substantial changes, amounting to a revision of the plan, must be referred to decision-makers. Continuous minor revisions are to be preferred where possible, since the attempt to make more substantial changes can lead to delays. However, there is no point in persisting with methods that are clearly failing to achieve their objectives.

This is the point at which benefits can be derived from the research initiated as part of, or in association with, the plan. If some of the problems encountered were anticipated, then research results may be available. This applies both to technical problems, for example of plant nutrition or water quality or social difficulties.

Where new problems arise, additional research will have to be undertaken.

There will usually be a change of emphasis over the lifetime of a development plan. In the beginning there will be an investment-intensive phase in which the results become visible in the shape of roads, water supplies, job opportunities, credit and material inputs. The second stage, consisting of extension and maintenance and operation of capital works, is harder to monitor. Day-to-day management is in the hands of individual farmers; credit repayments have to be administered, supplies of inputs maintained and marketing arrangements reviewed. The transition from the politically popular investment phase to the phase of ongoing maintenance and improvement is difficult. The latter calls for even more effective and willing cooperation between implementing agencies and land users.

CHECKLIST

Step 10

MONITORING AND REVISION

Responsibility: planning team

❏ List the goals and criteria achievement agreed in Step 1. Add any that emerged later in the planning period.

❏ Gather data relevant to each criterion of attainment: physical, economic and social.

❏ Compare what has been achieved with what was planned. Identify elements of success and failure.

❏ Seek explanations for failures. Were they caused by:
  – Incorrect assumptions of the plan?
  – Changed economic or political circumstances?
  – Logistic problems of implementation?
  – Problems of communication and participation?

❏ Review the goals: are they still valid?

❏ Initiate modification or revision of the plan:
  – minor modifications through action by implementing agencies;
  – larger revisions by the preparation of proposals and reference back to decision-makers.

Chapter 4
Methods and sources

A wide variety of methods are used in land-use planning They are taken from the natural sciences (climatology, soil science, ecology), from technology (agriculture, forestry, irrigation engineering) and from the social sciences (economics, sociology). Some of the methods, notably land evaluation, are interdisciplinary.

It is impossible to give detailed accounts of these methods in the guidelines. Many require handbooks of substantial length. The following notes indicate some of the principal sources in which such accounts can be found, details of which are given in the Bibliography, p. 93.

Land-use planning: general accounts

- Beatty, Peterson and Swindale (1978): the focus is on planning in developed countries.
- Davidson (1980): soils and land-use planning.
- FAO (1991b): includes accounts of 13 land-use planning applications, mainly in developing countries.
- ILRI (1980): includes detailed checklists of possible activities in regional planning.
- Laconte and Haimes (1985): water resources and land-use planning.

National land-use planning handbooks

National handbooks vary in content. Some are strongly focused on soil conservation, others include elements of land evaluation. Some examples are:
- Bangladesh: Brammer (1983).
- Brazil: Ramalho Filho *et al.* (1978).
- Canada: Lang and Armour (1980).
- Colombia: Vargas (1992).
- Ethiopia: FAO (1984b).
- Lesotho: Greenhow (1991).
- Sri Lanka: Dent and Ridgway (1986).
- United Republic of Tanzania: Corker (1983).
- Zimbabwe: Zimbabwe Federal Department of Conservation and Extension (1989).

Land-use planning applications
- OAS (1984): regional development planning.
- FAO (1991b): includes accounts of 13 land-use planning applications.

Information management

Decision-making depends on timely information on the present land-use situation, on possible ways of improving this situation and on the consequences of implementing each alternative solution. The gathering and storing of data requires much time in planning, but is not an end in itself. It is important to reserve time to interpret and apply these data to the task in hand. To manage information effectively, it is essential to know the place of each operation in the information system as a whole (Fig. 15). Otherwise, it is easy to concentrate on one part of the system, or one specialist task, without recognizing the implications it has for the whole operation. For example, if a lot of information is required, then a big investment in data collection, storage and reporting is necessary.

Good information management involves keeping a balance in the system. Information needs should drive data collection. Therefore, if there is a problem with grazing or drainage, focus attention there. Only collect data if it is known what they will be used for.

There must often be a trade-off between the excellence of the data and the time and cost of collecting them. Ways of making surveys cost effective include:
- Establish what is already available but check the reliability of the data.
- Collect data incrementally. Begin with a rapid overview of the whole area. Use this to identify those areas from which more detail is needed.
- Stratify the planning area. Divide the planning area according to the kind of informa-

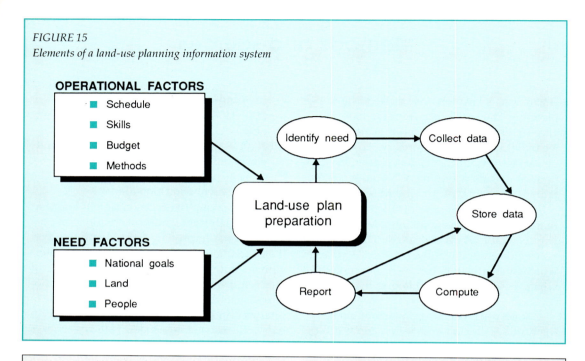

FIGURE 15
Elements of a land-use planning information system

Box 10
Questions on the use of computerized methods of information management

Any organization contemplating the introduction of computer assistance for natural resources surveys, land evaluation and land-use planning should seriously consider at least the following ten questions (Burrough, 1986):

1. Identify your problems carefully. What do your customers or users expect of you and will a computer help provide the service they need?
2. How much money have you for investment and operation?
3. Have you trained staff available to operate the computer or to ensure the strict organization that efficient use of a computer requires?
4. Are you aiming at countrywide systems or a single-project system?
5. How much data and what kinds of data will you have to process at any one time?
6. What is the structure of your data? Will you have to interface with other types of data that may possibly have a different organization?

7. What is the quality of graphic output you can afford and what quality will your staff and clients accept?
8. Have you the necessary physical support facilities such as stable electricity supplies, air-conditioning and low-humidity rooms?
9. Can you collect data that are of a reasonable quality and worth the investment of a computer system?
10. What existing systems can you make use of? Can you acquire them in a modular way, allowing the gradual buildup of a comprehensive computer system? How permanent are those systems and how dependent will you be on a particular company or supplier for support when things go wrong or become obsolete?

   A computer may not be necessary or cost effective. For small projects, it certainly will not. The most critical problem is likely to be the availability of trained staff.

tion needed. This may reflect the potential land-use pattern or a physical characteristic that may be a limiting factor; for example in hill country, where land use is limited by steep slopes, detailed soil information may not be needed. Usually, the land mapping units delineated in Step 3 will provide a basis for stratification.

- Carry out a pilot study. Work through the whole planning process, or at least Steps 3 to 6, for a small representative area. This will identify more clearly the relationships between the collaborating workers and agencies. Discussions between all parties will be more fruitful when the output of several steps is available. For example, financial analysts may not be very clear about what natural resource information they require for a specific project until they have had experience in using it.
- Know the method of analysis. Design each survey with the method of analysis to be used in mind.
- Organize and store the data systematically, paying attention to:
  - *Quality control.* Always list where and how data were obtained, in the field or from printed sources;
  - *Protection.* If stored on paper, protect from fire, damp and insects; if stored on computer diskettes, keep backups, both on diskette and as printouts; prevent unauthorized people altering data;
  - *Updating.* Record when data were last revised or updated.

Systems analysis

Data are often processed by means of systems analysis; that is, the analysis and modelling of interrelated processes. A system to be modelled must have defined boundaries. Within the system there are often stores of flows (of materials, energy, money, etc.). External flows cross the system boundaries as inputs and outputs. For example, in modelling nutrient dynamics in a plant-soil system, stores of nutrients occur in the plants, the organic soil fraction and the mineral soil fraction; internal flows refer, for example, to litter fall, humification and plant uptake from soil; and external flows to inputs such as atmospheric nitrogen fixation and outputs such as harvest of crops, or to the loss of nutrients in eroded soil. In modelling a farming system, some of the flows will refer to materials, such as seed and fertilizers, and others to energy or money.

Accounts of systems analysis, its potential and problems are given in:
- Arnold and Bennett (1975).
- Bennett and Thomas (1982).
- Biswas (1982).
- IIASA (1980).
- Morris (1977).
- National Research Council (1976).
- Quade and Miser (1982).
- Romero and Rehman (1989).
- Rossmiller (1978).

Geographic information systems

A geographic information system (GIS) is a computer-based system of storage and manipulation of data which is organized by area or location. Areas can be identified by a grid of cells (cell-based or raster systems), or information can be stored by means of the boundaries of mapped areas, e.g. land units or administrative units (polygon-based systems). A GIS enables different kinds of information to be recalled and combined; for example, areas that are both suitable for export crops and within a specified distance of an all-weather road could be overlain and mapped.

Most kinds of data processing undertaken on a GIS can also be done manually, by overlay of transparent maps, comparison and calculation. For small areas and few mapping units, this is the quickest way to do it. A GIS becomes efficient where there are numerous mapping units and many combinations of data are needed.

A GIS can offer valuable facilities to land-use planners. First, disaggregated data can be stored and retrieved by location. For example, crop yields may have been collected in order to calculate a financial measure of performance like the gross margin; these data can be stored and subsequently retrieved and used again for other purposes. Point data can be stored as such, rather than being lost by incorporation into mapping units. Thus, in a soil survey, data such as soil depth and texture, gathered for individual locations in the field, can be stored and retrieved for use in land evaluation. A further facility is to undertake complex and manually tedious calculations using any combination of the data in store. In this way, tables and maps of interpreted information can be produced very quickly. More important, the data can be updated or corrected and the methods of calculation revised by changing the computer program so that new maps and tables can be produced rapidly.

The cost of a GIS is now low and quite powerful systems can be run on personal computers. Systems have been developed for land-use planning, ranging from those that are relatively simple and easy to use (e.g. Ridgway and Jayasinghe, 1986) to complex ones (e.g. Wood and Dent, 1983; Schultink, 1987).

Accounts of the nature and potential of GISs are given in Burrough (1986) and Maguire, Goodchild and Rhind (1991). The IDRISI system is relatively easy to use and its capacity is

substantial. The CRIES system (Schultink, 1987) and the ILWIS system (Valenzuela, 1988) are specifically designed for land resource evaluation. A powerful but very complex system is ARC/INFO.

Natural resource surveys

There is a large number of publications on the survey of natural or environmental resources: following is a selection.

- Bunting (1987): a collection of methods that have been used for agro-ecological characterization and classification; see especially the chapters by Young (1987) and Brinkman (1987).
- Dent and Young (1981): an account of soil survey methods, suited to different scales and purposes, and of land evaluation, including a comparison of the FAO framework with other methods.
- FAO (1979b): soil survey methods for irrigation planning.
- FAO (1984c, 1987): agroclimatological data for Africa and Asia, respectively.
- Landon (1991): a useful reference for many aspects of soil evaluation and classification.
- Carver (1981): air photography in land-use planning.

Box 11
Climatic data for land-use planning

LAND QUALITIES
- Sufficiency of energy
- Frost hazard

- Sufficiency of water

- Irrigation need/drought hazard
- Length of growing season
- Hazard of high winds, high temperature, hail, low humidity
- Erosion hazard

CLIMATIC CHARACTERISTICS
- Temperature regime, sunshine hours, day length
- Probability of frost (local occurrence – not adequately recorded in standard data)
- Reference evaporation E_o
  Crop water requirement = E_o x crop coefficient
  Rainfall probability
  Effective rainfall
- Rainfall probability – crop water requirement
- Period of energy and water sufficiency
- Probability of occurrence in the growing season

- Rainfall intensity

- Lindgren (1985): applications of remote sensing methods in land-use planning.

The Agricultural Studies Unit of CIAT has created land system and agroclimatic databases to support agricultural research management. These and complementary agronomic techniques help CIAT in the selection of high-yielding crop varieties with farm-effective organic and mineral fertilizer recommendations for a given ecosystem, while contributing to the successful conservation and use of soil resources in tropical South America (Cochrane *et al.*, 1984).

Rural land-use analysis

Three methods have been described for the analysis of problems of rural land use: farming systems analysis, diagnosis and design and rapid rural appraisal. These have much in common: all are centred on interviews with a sample of rural land users, preferably stratified according to identified classes of farming system. The methods are not confined to problem diagnosis but include elements of later steps in land-use planning, particularly the design of improved land-use types and social analysis.

Farming systems analysis. (Fresco *et al.*, 1992; FAO, 1991b, p. 147-152.) This is centred on the identification of farm-level constraints and aims to develop adapted technologies for specific farming systems. The publications cited outline how it can be combined with land evaluation as an integrated sequence, i.e. land evaluation and farming systems analysis (LEFSA).

Diagnosis and design (D&D). (Raintree, 1987a; Young, 1986.) This approach was developed specifically for the design of agroforestry systems but can be applied to other types of land use. Diagnosis means the identification of problems with land-use systems and the analysis of their causes; design is the formulation of promising land-use types that might help solve these problems. The analogy is with the medical profession where a doctor must diagnose an illness before it can be treated. One way in which diagnosis and design can be integrated with

land evaluation procedures is given in Young (1986).

Rapid rural appraisal. (Abel *et al.*, 1989; FAO, 1989a; McCracken, Pretty and Conway, 1988). This approach is intended as a relatively rapid way of acquiring (in a matter of weeks) essential information on existing rural land-use systems, including the problems they entail.

Modelling

There is a large and increasing number of computer models relevant to different aspects of land-use planning. Most models consist essentially of quantitative predictions based on input data, for example the prediction of plant evapotranspiration from weather data or the prediction of net present return from data on inputs, production, costs and prices. Note that:

- models are only as reliable as the data which are entered into them;
- wherever possible, models should be calibrated for the planning area, its climate, soil types, etc.; data should be entered and the

---

Box 12
Water resource data for land-use planning

- Present water use
  - River abstraction, tanks, groundwater
  - Location of abstraction points, sluices, dams, wells and boreholes, with yields
- Present storage capacity of tanks and reservoirs
- Reliable yield of water for each river catchment – 75% and 90% probability low flow (from hydrograph records) or 75% and 90% probability rainfall – E_o over seven- or ten-day day periods x area of catchment
- Safe yield of groundwater (from test pump data or well records)
- Depth below surface of useful groundwater
- Location of aquifers
- Water quality
- Location of irrigable land
- Legal and customary rights

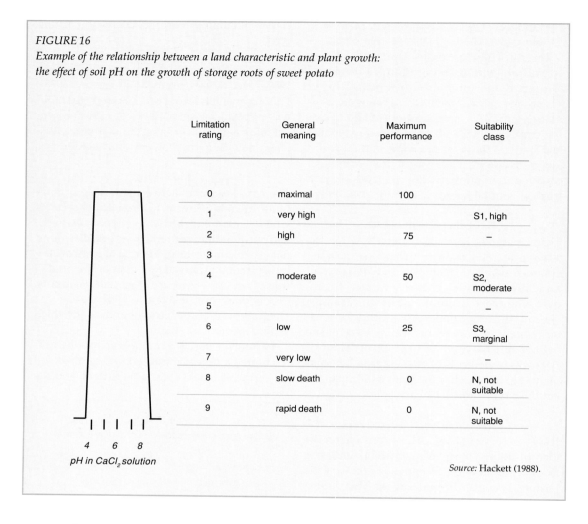

FIGURE 16

Example of the relationship between a land characteristic and plant growth:
the effect of soil pH on the growth of storage roots of sweet potato

Limitation rating	General meaning	Maximum performance	Suitability class
0	maximal	100	
1	very high		S1, high
2	high	75	–
3			
4	moderate	50	S2, moderate
5			–
6	low	25	S3, marginal
7	very low		–
8	slow death	0	N, not suitable
9	rapid death	0	N, not suitable

pH in CaCl$_2$ solution

Source: Hackett (1988).

results compared with an independent measure, for instance crop yield.

Results from modelling can be combined with a GIS to show the spatial extent of the effects modelled (e.g. crop yield, tree growth).

Examples of the purposes for which modelling has been applied in land-use planning are:

- Agriculture (Heady and Srivastara, 1975).
- Crop growth, for example the CERES/DSSAT set of models (Jones and Kiniry, 1986); WOFOST (van Diepen *et al.*, 1988).
- Crop water requirements (FAO, 1977; 1979a).
- Decision-making in land-use planning

(Cocks *et al.*, 1983; Ive, 1984; Ive and Cocks, 1987).

- Forestry and agroforestry (Davey, Prinsley and White, 1991).
- Land evaluation, e.g. automated physical land evaluation (APLE); automated land evaluation system (ALES) (Beek, Burrough and McCormack, 1987; Higgins *et al.*, 1987; van Keulen *et al.*, 1987).
- Soil erosion, e.g. the universal soil loss equation (USLE) (Wischmeier and Smith, 1978); soil loss estimator for southern Africa (SLEMSA) (Elwell and Stocking, 1982).
- Soil response to land use, e.g. soil changes

under agroforestry (SCUAF) (Young and Muraya, 1990); CENTURY (Parton *et al.*, 1989).

- Descriptions of a range of models applicable, with references, are found in Bunting (1987) and Davey, Prinsley and White (1991).

Land evaluation

Land evaluation in its broad sense covers Steps 1 to 6 in Chapter 3, from the setting of goals to land suitability evaluation, including environmental, economic and social analysis. It has been most widely applied as qualitative (physical) land evaluation, as in Step 5. Among the information to be found in land evaluation handbooks are checklists of descriptors for land-use types, land qualities and land characteristics as relevant to different kinds of land use.

The basis of the approach is described in FAO (1976). Other accounts are given in Dent and Young (1981) and McCrae and Burnham (1981). Recent developments in quantitative land evaluation, including computer programs and modelling, are described in Beek, Burrough and McCormack (1987). Detailed guidelines are available on land evaluation for:

- rain-fed agriculture (FAO, 1983);
- irrigated agriculture (FAO, 1985a);
- forestry (FAO, 1984a);
- extensive grazing (FAO, 1991b).

Requirements for plant growth

The FAO Soil Resources, Management and Conservation Service is establishing a two-level database (ECOCROP 1 and 2) covering the ecological requirements and responses of plants, with emphasis on economic crops. ECOCROP 1 which, by July 1993, contained data for 1 200 species, identifies arable crop, pasture and tree species for defined environments.

In ECOCROP 2, designed to support a wide range of existing and future models, information is held in the form of pairs of coordinates representing the response of a whole plant or plant process at a given level of an environmental factor, with specified values for the other factors. For example, growth rate at a given temperature or rate of photosynthesis at a given light intensity. The aim will be to have at least three or four of such pairs in order to define a response curve.

At an intermediate level, empirical relationships for plant/environment response have been collected for a large number of plants by Hackett (1988).

Some countries have begun to collect data on plant growth requirements at a national level under the direction of national soil survey or land-use planning organizations. Other local systems will be found in previous land evaluation surveys. Criteria should not be taken uncritically from previous surveys but rather examined and, if possible, tested.

Financial and economic analysis

Financial and economic analysis for the purpose of land-use planning uses essentially the same basic methods as do other kinds of project analysis. The foundation of this method is set out in Gittinger (1982) and Bridger and Wipenny (1983). The application of economic analysis to natural resources is discussed in Pearce and Turner (1990), Wipenny (1991) and Whitby and Willis (1978).

A specific problem encountered is that of choosing the discount rate for investments of which the returns will not be received for many years, e.g. most kinds of forestry. This is discussed by Leslie (1987). The application of economics to land-use planning is discussed in Harrison (1977).

Decision-making

- Romero and Rehman (1989).

People's participation

- Huizer (1983).

Land tenure

- FAO (1989b): appraisal of tree and land tenure.
- Raintree (1987b): land and tree tenure in agroforestry.

•Dale and McLaughlin (1988): cadastral aspects of land-use planning.

Implementation

•Mollett (1984).

Legislation for land use

•FAO (1971).
•Roberts (1977).
•FAO (1985b).

Glossary

Agroclimatic region
An area of land that is suited to a specified range of crops, defined in terms of its temperature and rainfall regimes and, especially, its **growing period**.

Agro-ecosystem
An **ecosystem** based on agriculture. A farm, or component of a farm, treated as an ecosystem.

Agroforestry
A collective name for land-use systems in which woody perennials (trees, shrubs, etc.) are grown in association with herbaceous plants (crops, pastures) and/or livestock, in a spatial arrangement, a rotation or both, and in which there are both ecological and economic interactions between the tree and non-tree components of the system.

Air photographs
Photographs of the land surface taken from aircraft, usually at a vertical angle, normally at scales of from 1:50 000 to 1:5 000. For interpretation, air photographs are viewed stereoscopically to give a three-dimensional impression. Landforms, vegetation, land use and some infrastructure (especially roads and tracks) can be directly seen on air photographs, while soil properties, geology and other land properties require indirect interpretation and administrative boundaries cannot be seen. Air photographs can also be used as base maps for presentation of a land-use plan. Air photographs may be panchromatic (black and white), colour (true colour) or false colour (see **false colour imagery**). Also called aerial photographs.

Aquaculture
Management of any plant or animal that lives in water, e.g. fish farming, shrimp farming.

Note: For terms in bold, see separate entries.

Benefit-cost ratio
The **present value** of the benefits from an enterprise (farm, forest, etc.) divided by the present value of its costs.

Cadastral survey
The inventory and register of landownership on maps.

Conservation requirements
The conditions of land necessary or desirable to achieve conservation of natural resources under a given **land-use type**.

Critical path method
A way of planning the operations needed to complete a land-use planning project by identifying the individual operations needed and plotting how each task has to be related to the others in time.

Crop requirements
The conditions of land necessary or desirable for the successful growth of a crop.

Decision-maker
An executive person or group responsible for land-use policy, action and allocation of resources.

Digitized map
Mapped information stored in numerical form as a series of coordinates (north, east) and their values or properties (e.g. altitude, soil series, land use).

Discounted cash flow analysis
A method of **financial analysis** and **economic analysis** in which future benefits and future costs are reduced to a lower value, which is judged to be their **present value**, by **discounting**.

Discounting
The reverse of adding interest. The value of a cost incurred, or benefit received, is reduced by an annual percentage, i.e. the **discount rate**, to obtain its **present value**.

Discount rate
The interest rate used to assess the **present value** of a future value by **discounting**. To simulate the investment behaviour in the private sector, the discount rate is set equal to the required rate of return in that sector. To calculate the **social value** of benefits and costs, an appropriate **social discount rate** should be used.

Diagnosis and design
An approach to, and set of methods for, the diagnosis of problems of land-use systems and the design of improved land-use systems which will help to solve these problems. Originally developed for the design of agroforestry systems, but can be applied to other kinds of land use. Also referred to as D&D.

District-level land-use planning
A level of land-use planning between the national and local levels, typically but not necessarily that of the administrative district. Intermediate **map scales** are used. Land-use development projects are often at the district level. (See **local-level land-use planning** and **national-level land-use planning**.)

Ecosystem
A functioning, interacting system composed of living organisms and their environment. The concept is applicable at any scale, from the planet as an ecosystem to a microscopic colony of organisms and its immediate surroundings.

Economic analysis
Analysis that views the money value of a land-use system for the community as a whole.

Emergency planning
Land-use planning in response to a perceived problem for which action is urgently needed.

Environmental impact analysis
A procedure to predict the effects of changes in land use on the environment, particularly effects on water, soils, vegetation and human health and well-being.

Erosion hazard
The risk of **soil erosion** occurring under specified conditions, or in a specified area. Erosion hazard may be expressed in qualitative terms (severe, moderate, slight, etc.) or quantitative terms (as predicted soil loss in tonnes per hectare per year).

False colour imagery
Special film which records infrared radiation (which is not visible) as if it were red light; to make room for the infrared, the visible colours are moved across the spectrum so that red light is recorded as green and green as blue. False colour film can be used in air photographs or satellite imagery. False colour is valuable in distinguishing different kinds of vegetation and crops, as living vegetation contains chlorophyll which reflects infrared radiation strongly.

Farming system
A class consisting of all farms with similar land use, environment and economy; comprising the farm household, its land and the systems of cropping or livestock production for consumption or sale. A farming system is a decision-making unit and a **land-use system** based on agriculture.

Farming systems analysis Investigation of farm-level constraints, translation of this knowledge into improved technology and testing of this technology.

Financial analysis
Analysis which looks at the money value of a system to the farmer, other land-user or private investor.

Geographic information system (GIS)
A computer system for storage, analysis and

retrieval of information, in which all data are spatially referenced by their geographic coordinates (north, east). In addition to primary data, such as climatic and soil characteristics, a GIS can be used to calculate derived values, such as erosion hazard, forest yield class, or land suitability for specified land-use types. Data are usually derived from maps and derived values can be printed out as maps.

Goal

One of the major objectives of a land-use plan, defined in generalized terms, often those of policy.

Gross margin analysis

The calculation of the annual income of a single enterprise by taking the value of sales and subtracting the variable costs of production to obtain a margin of profit or loss.

Growing period

A continuous period of the year during which temperature and soil water availability are sufficiently high to permit plant growth. In most of the tropics, the growing period is determined by water availability within rooting depth in the soil. In the temperate zone, low temperature is often limiting. In areas with bimodal rainfall distribution there may be two growing periods each year. The term applies primarily to annual crops, since deep-rooted trees can continue to grow when the top 2 m or more of soil is dry.

Incremental planning

Land-use planning based on small improvements to land-use systems, made one at a time.

Information management

Gathering, storing and analysing information needed for a specific purpose, such as land-use planning.

Infrastructure

Permanent installations constructed to assist economic activity, such as roads, irrigation or drainage works, buildings and communication systems.

Integrated survey

See **land systems survey**.

Internal rate of return

A financial or economic indicator of the net benefits expected from a project or enterprise, expressed as a percentage. In **financial analysis,** the internal rate of return can be compared with the rate of interest prevalent in the market.

Land

An area of the earth's surface, including all elements of the physical and biological environment that influence land use. Thus land refers not only to soil but also landforms, climate, hydrology, vegetation and fauna, together with *land improvements* such as terraces and drainage works.

Land capability classification

A classification of land in terms of its potential for use in specified ways and with specified management practices, generally as a sequence of capability classes 1, 2, 3... (or I, II, III...). Class 1 is treated as the "best" land, being suited to most types of use, while successively higher-numbered classes have more limitations and less flexibility of use. The United States Department of Agriculture's land capability classification is the best known, but adaptations to other countries have been made. The approach is different from that of **land suitability** evaluation, although the two can be reconciled.

Land characteristic

An attribute of land that can be measured or estimated, for example slope angle, soil depth or mean annual rainfall.

Land evaluation

The assessment of the suitability of land for specified uses. Assessment is made in terms of production, **sustainability**, the inputs needed to obtain that production, and (in the case of quantitative **land suitability classification**), economic return.

Land facet
A subdivision of a **land system**, consisting of an area of land which is fairly uniform with respect to properties that affect land use, e.g. has a narrow range of slope angle or soil type.

Land information system
A collection of information relevant to suitability for land use, particularly **land characteristics**. Land information systems are generally, but not necessarily, stored in **geographic information systems**.

Land quality
A complex attribute of land which affects its suitability for specific uses in a distinct way. For example, the land quality "availability of water" directly affects crop yields and, therefore, land suitability for different crops. Most land qualities can only be assessed by modelling the interaction of a number of **land characteristics**. For example, availability of water is modelled from data on rainfall, available water capacity of the soil, potential evapotranspiration.

Land tenure
The ownership or leasing system of land, or of the rights to use it.

Landsat
A United States series of earth resource satellites first launched in 1972. Systematic, repeated digital data on the reflectance of, or radiation from, the earth's surface are acquired, and these can be interpreted in terms of **land characteristics**. Data are collected separately for different visible and invisible wavebands, which can be combined for interpretation. Under favourable conditions, the ground resolution can reach 30 m. Compare **Spot**.

Land suitability
The fitness of land for a specified kind of use.

Land suitability class
One of a set of classes for evaluating **land suitability**. The FAO system consists of three levels of classification: suitable or not suitable (S or N); degrees of suitability, e.g. highly, moderately or marginally suitable (S1, S2 or S3); and a letter indicating the major land **limitation** that has led to the class allocation (e.g. S2w = water limitation, S2e = erosion hazard limitation. (See Table 5, p. 40.)

Land system
An area of land with a recurring pattern of landforms, soils and vegetation and having a relatively uniform climate. Alternatively defined as an area of land with a recurring pattern of **land facets**.

Land systems survey
A survey of land resources based on mapping of **land systems**; usually **land facets** are also either identified or mapped. Otherwise called **integrated survey**.

Land unit
An area of land which possesses specific **land characteristics** and **land qualities** and which can be mapped.

Land use
The management of land to meet human needs. This includes **rural land use** and also urban and industrial use.

Land-use plan
A coherent set of decisions about the use of land and ways to achieve the desired use. A land-use plan includes: a definition of goals; an ordering of land and human and material resources; an explicit statement of the methods, organization, responsibilities and schedule to be used; and agreed targets.

Land-use planning
The systematic assessment of land and water potential, alternative patterns of land use and other physical, social and economic conditions,

for the purpose of selecting and adopting land-use options which are most beneficial to land users without degrading the resources or the environment, together with the selection of measures most likely to encourage such land uses. Land-use planning may be at international, national, district (project, catchment), or local (village) levels. (See district-, **local-** and **national-level land-use planning.**) It includes participation by **land users**, **planners** and **decision-makers** and covers educational, legal, fiscal and financial measures.

Land-use requirement
Land conditions necessary or desirable for the successful and sustained practice of a given **land-use type**. Includes **crop requirements** or **plant growth requirements**, management requirements and **conservation requirements**.

Land users
All people who obtain their livelihood directly, either wholly or partly, from the land, e.g. farmers, foresters, pastoralists, staff of national parks.

Land-use system
A specific **land-use type** applied to a particular area of **land**.

Land-use type
A kind of land use described in enough detail to assess its **land-use requirements** and to plan the necessary inputs. The amount of detail varies with the level, scale and purposes of the survey, from generalized land-use types, such as "dairy farming" or "irrigated agriculture" in reconnaissance surveys, to detailed descriptions of plants, management, inputs, etc. in more intensive surveys.

Levels of land-use planning
The scale and intensity of a land-use plan, which may be at the national, district or local level.

Limiting value
The value of a **land quality**, or **land character-istics**, identified as marking the boundary between **land suitability classes**.

Limitation
A **land quality**, or **land characteristic**, which adversely affects the potential of land for a specified kind of use, e.g. salinity, storm damage hazard.

Local-level land-use planning
Planning based on a village or other local community. Large **map scales** are used, such as 1:10 000. Also referred to as **village level land-use planning**.

Logistic planning
Planning for the arrangement of inputs (capital and recurrent) and supplies, personnel and scheduling, for land use or for the implementation of a land-use plan.

Map scale
The ratio between distances on the ground and distances on a map. Small scales refer to maps which cover a large area such as a country on one map sheet, e.g. a scale of 1:1 000 000. Large scales refer to maps which cover a small area on one map sheet, e.g. a scale of 1:10 000.

Matching
This term is used in two ways. In its narrower sense, the process of comparing land-use requirements with **land qualities** or **land characteristics**, to arrive at a **land suitability classification**. In its broader sense, the process of adaptation of **land-use types**, and consideration of land improvements, so as to arrive at land-use types which are better suited to the land.

Modelling
The construction of physical, conceptual or mathematical simulations of the real world. Models help to show relationships between processes (physical, economic or social) and may be used to predict the effects of changes in land use.

Monitoring
The collection of information for the purpose of assessment of the progress and success of a land-use plan. Monitoring is used for the purpose of revising the original plan or to gather experience for future plans.

National-level land-use planning
Applied to planning at national government level which deals with the country's land, water or other resources as a whole. Small **map scales** are used. In large countries, planning of the major administrative divisions has some of the characteristics of national-level planning.

Natural resources
The resources of the land relevant to its potential for land use, e.g. climate, water, soils, pastures, forests.

Net present value
The **present value** of the benefits of an enterprise minus the present value of its costs.

Objective
A specific aim, expressing something to be achieved as part of the goals of a land-use plan.

On-farm research
Experimental work conducted on farms. There is a spectrum of research types, ranging from researcher-managed to farmer-managed.

On-station research
Experimental work conducted on experimental stations.

Partial farm budget
A budget of only part of a farm enterprise, assuming that only certain elements will change while the remainder will be constant; for example, the budget of a dairy enterprise on a mixed arable-dairy farm. It compares the marginal cost of an activity within the enterprise with the marginal increase in benefit that the activity will bring. Distinguished from **whole farm budget**.

Planner, planners, planning team
The person or group responsible for the preparation of a land-use plan, working in close cooperation with the **land users** and the **decision-makers**.

Planning
The exercise of foresight, systematically examining alternative proposals for action to attain specified **goals** and **objectives**. Includes the description of the desired future state of affairs and of the actions needed to bring about this state.

Plant growth requirements
The conditions of land necessary for the successful growth of a plant. The same as **crop requirements**, except that plant growth requirement applies to any plant, not necessarily an agricultural crop.

Present value
The value of an enterprise at the present time, after applying the process of discounting to its costs or benefits.

Program
The standard spelling of a computer program.

Programme
A set of interactive, synchronized activities or **projects** aimed at achieving defined objectives by means of ongoing activities.

Project
A set of activities with defined **objectives** to be completed in a certain time span.

Qualitative land suitability classification
Land suitability classification in which the results are expressed in qualitative terms only, without specific estimates of inputs, outputs or costs and returns. The description "qualitative" refers to the results of the suitability classification, not the conduct of the land evaluation.

Quantitative land suitability classification
Land suitability classification in which the results are expressed in numerical terms which permit comparison between suitabilities for different kinds of use. Usually these are economic terms, but quantitative physical comparisons are possible between uses with the same objective, e.g. between different pasture systems in terms of livestock carrying capacity or different forestry systems in terms of wood production.

Rapid rural appraisal
An exploratory survey procedure carried out by a multidisciplinary team to gain a quick overview of a local land-use situation. It involves review of existing data, remote sensing, field observation and interviews with **land users**, local government officials and others; it may cover both physical and socio-economic aspects.

Remote sensing
In land-use planning, remote sensing refers to the gathering of information through the use of **air photograph**s and **satellite imagery**. Remote sensing should be conducted in conjunction with field surveying on the ground.

Research
A set of activities directed towards the advancement of knowledge. Applied in land-use planning to improvements in the performance or management of land-use types (e.g. by better crop varieties, better scheduling of irrigation water), or to the prevention of problems encountered (e.g. pests and diseases). Experimental research may be **on-station** or **on-farm research**.

Risk analysis
An analytical technique in which the probabilities of occurrence of an adverse event (e.g. drought, hurricane, drop in the market price of a product) are estimated for each critical element of a project. Repeated calculations (normally by computer) are then made of a measure of the value of the project, with each element entering into successive computations according to the probability of its occurrence.

Rural land use
Land use other than urban and industrial use. Including agriculture (rain-fed and irrigated), livestock production, forestry, **agroforestry**, **aquaculture**, wildlife conservation, recreation and tourism.

Satellite imagery
Remote sensing imagery gathered by earth-orbiting satellites, including **Landsat** and **Spot**. Images are in specific wavebands (visible, infrared, etc.), which may be combined for purposes of interpretation. Images look like photographs but are not obtained by photographic methods, hence the term "images" or "imagery". Data from satellite imagery can be interpreted visually or analysed by computers in digitized form; they can also be entered directly into **geographic information systems**.

Sectoral agencies
Government departments or other agencies with a limited, specific field of responsibility, e.g. ministries or departments of agriculture, forestry, veterinary services, or a water or irrigation authority.

Sensitivity analysis
An analytical technique to deal with uncertainty about future events and values. It consists of varying one element (e.g. rainfall, market price), or a combination of elements, and determining the effect of those changes on the outcome of a project. In economic analysis, the effect of the changes on a measure of project value is calculated.

Shadow price
In economic analysis, this is any distortion of a free market price which is made in order to reflect the real scarcity value of goods or services, including labour. An example of a shadow price is the elimination of the effect of taxes or subsidies.

Social analysis The analysis of a plan in terms of its impact of different sections of the community. Social analysis gives particular attention to the interests of minority groups, women and the poor.

Social discount rate
The **discount rate** used to estimate the social value (or value to the community as a whole) of an enterprise. It is sometimes held that, to reflect social values, the social discount rate should be lower than the discount rate used in the private sector.

Soil conservation
Activities aimed at minimizing the loss of soil by erosion. Soil conservation can be achieved by earth structures, such as banks and ditches, or by biological means, particularly maintaining a soil cover of living plants or plant litter. Soil conservation is also used in a wider sense to refer to all activities aimed at conserving the fertility of the soil.

Soil erosion
Removal of soil by wind, water or landsliding at a substantially faster rate than that at which soil-forming processes can replace it. Soil erosion is a result of human activities such as clearance of vegetation and cultivation of sloping land without adequate **soil conservation** measures.

Soil landscape
A soil mapping unit defined by its landform pattern and associated soils.

Soil mapping unit
Any unit describing the spatial distribution of soils, which can be mapped. Soil mapping units may be simple, consisting of one type of soil, or complex, consisting of two or more types of soil.

Soil profile
A vertical section through the soil, as seen in a soil pit. Usually, this reveals several more or less distinct soil horizons which differ in colour, texture and other properties.

Spot
(Satellite probatoire d'observation de la terre.) A French series of earth resource satellites, first launched in 1986. Under favourable conditions, the ground resolution can reach 10 m. Compare **Landsat**.

Standard
In land-use planning, standards refer to planning guidelines or limits, including conservation standards, standards for land-use management, standards for construction of capital works or standards for economic measures, e.g. loan interest rates.

Steeplands
Areas in which the slopes are predominantly steep or moderately steep and which therefore have distinctive land-use problems, e.g. high erosion hazard, landsliding and difficulty of road construction.

Strategy
The logical framework for coordinating decisions that link development **goals** with the actions intended to achieve those goals.

Sustainability
See **sustainable land use**.

Sustainable land use
The central concept underlying use of this term is production combined with conservation. Alternative definitions are:
- land use which maintains production at or above its present level while, at the same time, conserving the natural resources (water, soil, pastures, forests, etc.) on which that production depends;
- land use which does not progressively degrade its productive capacity;
- land use which meets the needs of the present while at the same time conserving resources for future generations (WCED, 1987).

The achievement of sustainable land use is not confined to technical measures, but includes the economic and social conditions necessary for the success of these. The term **sustainability** is used in more or less the same sense.

System
A functional arrangement of components that process inputs into outputs, for example a farm. Systems display properties which result from the interaction of their components.

Systems analysis
The analysis and **modelling** of interrelated processes and operations with a view to designing a more efficient use of resources.

Tree tenure
The ownership, or rights to the use, of trees. Tree tenure is sometimes different from land tenure.

Variable costs
In financial analysis, the costs of production that can be attributed specifically to the activity being analysed. For example, in wheat production, the costs of seed, fertilizer, cultivation and harvesting are specific to the wheat crop and, therefore, form its variable costs.

Village-level land-use planning
An alternative term for **local-level land-use planning**.

Wetlands
Areas that are frequently flooded or waterlogged and so possess a distinct ecosystem adapted to a high water-table, e.g. a saltmarsh, a mangrove swamp or freshwater fen.

Whole farm budget
A budget of an entire farm enterprise. Distinguished from **partial farm budget**.

Bibliography

Abel, N.O.J., Drinkwater, M.J., Ingram, J., Okafor, J. & Prinsley, R.T. 1989. *Guidelines for training in rapid appraisal for agroforestry research and extension. Amelioration of soils by trees.* London, Commonwealth Science Council; Harare, Zimbabwe, Forestry Commission. 117 pp.

Arnold, G.W. & Bennett, D. 1975. The problem of finding an optimum solution. *In* G. E. Dalton, ed. *Study of agricultural systems,* p. 129-173. Barking, Essex, UK, Applied Science Publishers.

Beatty, M.T., Petersen, G.W. & Swindale, L.D., eds. 1978. *Planning the uses and management of land. Agronomy 21.* Madison, USA, Am. Soc. Agron. 1028 pp.

Beek, K.J., Burrough, P.A. & McCormack, D.E., eds. 1987. *Quantitative land evaluation procedures.* ITC Publication 6. Enschede, the Netherlands, ITC.

Bennett, D. & Thomas, J.F., eds. 1982. *On rational grounds: systems analysis in catchment land use.* Amsterdam, Elsevier.

Biswas, A.K. 1982. Water management: applying systems analysis in developing countries. *Ceres,* 15(6): 40-42.

Brammer, H. 1983. *Manual on Upazilla land use planning.* Dacca, Bangladesh, Ministry of Local Government, Rural Development and Cooperatives. 74 pp.

Bridger, G.A. & Wipenny, J.T. 1983. *Planning development projects: a practical guide to the choice and appraisal of public sector investments.* London, Overseas Development Administration. 209 pp.

Brinkman, R. 1987. Agro-ecological characterization, classification and mapping. Different approaches by the International Agricultural Research Centres. *In* A. H. Bunting, ed. *Agricultural environments: characterization, classification and mapping,* p. 31-42. Wallingford, UK, CAB International.

Bunting, A.H., ed. 1987. *Agricultural environments: characterization, classification and mapping.* Wallingford, UK, CAB International. 335 pp.

Burrough, P.A. 1986. *Principles of geographical information systems for land resources assessment.* Monographs on Soil and Resources Survey No. 12. Oxford, UK, Clarendon. 193 pp.

Carver, A. J. 1981. *Air photography for land use planners.* Harare, Zimbabwe, Department of Conservation and Extension. 76 pp.

Cochrane, T.T., Sánchez, L.G., de Azevedo, L.G., Porras, J.A. & Garver, C.L. 1984. *Land in tropical America,* Vol. 1. CIAT and EMBRAPA-CPAC. Cali, Colombia, CIAT 144 pp.

Cocks, K.D., Ive, J.R., Davis, J.P. & Baird, I.A. 1983. SIRO-PLAN and LUPLAN: an Australian approach to land use planning. *Environment and Planning,* B10 (3): 331-355.

Corker, I. 1983. *Land use planning handbook, Tanzania.* Surbiton, UK, Land Resources Development Centre, Overseas Development Administration. 178 pp.

Dale, P. F. & McLaughlin, J. D. 1988. *Land information management: an introduction with special reference to cadastral problems in Third World countries.* Oxford, UK, Clarendon.

Davey, S.M., Prinsley, R. & White, D.H., eds. 1991. Forestry and agroforestry. *Agric. Syst. Inf. Tech. Newsl.,* 3(3). Canberra, Australia, Bureau of Rural Resources.

Davidson, D.A. 1980. *Soils and land use planning.* London, Longman. 129 pp.

Dent, D.L. & Ridgway, R.B. 1986. *A land use planning handbook for Sri Lanka.* FD 2, SRL 79/058. Colombo, Sri Lanka, Land Use Policy Planning Division, Ministry of Lands and Land Development. 389 pp.

Dent, D. & Young, A. 1981. *Soil survey and land evaluation.* London, Allen and Unwin. 278 pp.

Elwell, H.A. & Stocking, M.A. 1982. Developing a simple yet practical method of soil-loss estimation. *Trop. Agric. (Trinidad),* 59: 43-48.

FAO. 1971. *Legislative principles of soil conservation.* FAO Soils Bulletin No. 15. Rome, FAO.

FAO. 1976. *A framework for land evaluation.* FAO Soils Bulletin No. 32. Rome, FAO. 72 pp. Also published as Publication 22. Wageningen, the Netherlands, ILRI. 87 pp.

FAO. 1977. *Crop water requirements.* FAO Irrigation and Drainage Paper No. 24. Rome, FAO. 144 pp.

FAO. 1979a. *Yield response to water.* FAO Irrigation and Drainage Paper No. 33. Rome, FAO. 144 pp.

FAO. 1979b. *Soil survey investigations for irrigation.* FAO Soils Bulletin No. 42. Rome, FAO, 188 pp.

FAO. 1983. *Guidelines: land evaluation for rainfed agriculture.* FAO Soils Bulletin No. 52. Rome, FAO. 237 pp.

FAO. 1984a. *Land evaluation for forestry.* FAO Forestry Paper No. 48. Rome, FAO. 123 pp.

FAO. 1984b. *Guidelines for land use planning, Ethiopia.* Assistance to Land Use Planning Project, FAO Technical Report No. 10. Rome, FAO. 160 pp.

FAO. 1984c. *Agroclimatological data for Africa,* Vols 1 and 2. FAO Plant Production and Protection Series No. 22. Rome, FAO.

FAO. 1985a. *Guidelines: land evaluation for irrigated agriculture.* FAO Soils Bulletin No. 55. Rome, FAO. 229 pp.

FAO. 1985b. *The role of legislation in land use planning for developing countries.* FAO Legislative Study No. 31. Rome, FAO. 160 pp.

FAO. 1987. *Agroclimatological data for Asia,* Vols 1 and 2. FAO Plant Production and Protection Series No. 23. Rome, FAO.

FAO. 1989a. *Community forestry rapid appraisal.* FAO Community Forestry Note No. 3. Rome, FAO. 90 pp.

FAO. 1989b. *Rapid appraisal of tree and land tenure.* FAO Community Forestry Note No. 5. Rome, FAO.

FAO. 1991a. *Guidelines: land evaluation for extensive grazing.* FAO Soils Bulletin No. 58. Rome, FAO. 158 pp.

FAO. 1991b. *Land use planning applications. Proceedings of the FAO Expert Consultation, 1990,* Rome, Italy, 10-14 December 1990. World Soil Resources Reports 68. Rome, FAO. 206 pp.

Fresco, L.O, Huizing, H.G.J., van Keulen, H., Luning, H.A. & Schipper, R.A. 1992. *Land evaluation and farming systems analysis for land use planning.* FAO/ITC/Wageningen Agricultural University. (unpubl. FAO Working Document)

Gittinger, J. P. 1982. *Economic analysis of agricultural projects,* 2nd ed. Baltimore, Johns Hopkins University Press. 505 pp.

Greenhow, T. 1991. *Lesotho community land use planning. A manual.* Maseru, Lesotho, Ministry of Agriculture and Marketing. 106 pp.

Hackett, C. 1988. *Matching plants and land.* Natural Resources Series No. 11. Canberra, Australia, CSIRO Division of Water and Land Resources. 82 pp.

Harrison, A.J. 1977. *Economics and land use planning.* London, Croom Helm. 250 pp.

Heady, E.O. & Srivastara, U.K. 1975. *Spatial sector programming models in agriculture.* Ames, Iowa State University Press.

Higgins, G.M., Kassam, A.H., van Velthuizen, H.T. & Purnell, M.F. 1987. Methods used by FAO to estimate environmental resources, potential outputs of crops and population-supporting capacities in the developing nations. *In* A.H. Bunting, ed. *Agricultural environments: characterization, classification and mapping,* p. 171-184. Wallingford, UK, CAB International.

Hill, I. D., ed. 1979. *Land resources of central Nigeria. Agricultural development possibilities.* Surbiton, UK, Land Resources Development

Centre, Overseas Development Administration.

Huizer, G. 1983. *Guiding principles for people's participation projects; design, operation, monitoring and ongoing evaluation.* Rome, FAO.

IIASA. 1980. *Beware the pitfalls. A short guide to avoiding common errors in systems analysis.* Executive Report 2. Laxenburg, Austria, International Institute for Applied Systems Analysis. 23 pp.

ILRI. 1980. *Framework for regional planning in developing countries.* ILRI Publication 26. Wageningen, the Netherlands, ILRI. 345 pp.

Ive, J.R. 1984. *LUPLAN: Microsoft BASIC, CP/M users manual.* Technical Memorandum 84/5, Canberra, Australia, CSIRO Division of Water and Land Resources.

Ive, J.R. & Cocks, K.D. 1987. The value of adding searching and profiling capabilities to a land use planning package. *Soil Survey and Land Evaluation,* 7: 87-94.

Jones, C.A. & Kiniry, J.R., eds. 1986. *CERES – Maize. A simulation model of maize growth and development.* College Station, Texas A&M University Press. 194 pp.

Laconte, P. & Haimes, Y.Y. 1985. *Water resources and land use planning; a systems approach.* NATO Advanced Studies Institute Series. The Netherlands, Nijhoff.

Landon, J.R., ed. 1991. *Booker tropical soil manual.* Harlow, UK, Longman. 474 pp.

Lang, R. & Armour, A. 1980. *Environmental planning resource book.* Canada, Lands Directorate. 355 pp.

Leslie, A.J. 1987. A second look at the economics of natural management systems in tropical mixed forests. *Unasylva,* 39: 47-58.

Lindgren, D.T. 1985. *Land use planning and remote sensing. Part II. Remote sensing input to GIS.* London, Nijhoff. 176 pp.

Maguire, D.J., Goodchild, M.F. & Rhind, D.W., eds. 1991. *Geographical information systems: principles and applications,* Vols 1 and 2. Harlow, UK, Longman.

McCracken, J.A., Pretty, J.N. & Conway, G.R. 1988. *An introduction to rapid rural appraisal for agricultural development.* London, IIED. 96 pp.

McCrae, S.G. & Burnham, C.P. 1981. *Land evaluation.* Oxford, UK, Clarendon. 239 pp.

Mollett, J.A. 1984. *Planning for agricultural development.* London, Croom Helm. 384 pp.

Morris, R.M. 1977. The systems approach in teaching resource planners. *Agric. Syst.,* 2: 227-238.

National Research Council. 1976. *Systems analysis and operations research; a tool for policy and program planning for developing countries.* Washington, DC, United States National Academy of Sciences. 98 pp.

OAS. 1984. *Integrated regional development planning; guidelines and case studies from OAS experience.* Department of Regional Development, Organization of American States in cooperation with United States National Park Service and USAID. 497 pp.

Parton, W.J., Sanford, R.L., Sanchez, P.A. & Stewart, J.W.B. 1989. Modelling soil organic matter dynamics in tropical soils. *In* D. C. Coleman, J. M. Oades & G. Uehara, eds. *Dynamics of soil organic matter in tropical ecosystems,* p. 153-171. Manoa, Hawaii, University of Hawaii.

Pearce, D.W. & Turner, R.K. 1990. *Economics of natural resources and the environment.* Baltimore, Johns Hopkins University Press. 373 pp.

Quade, S. & Miser, H.J. 1982. What is systems analysis? *Options,* 10-13. Laxenburg, Austria, International Institute for Applied Systems Analysis.

Raintree, J.B. 1987a. *D&D user's manual: an introduction to agroforestry diagnosis and design.* Nairobi, Kenya ICRAF. 110 pp.

Raintree, J.B. 1987b. *Land, trees and tenure.* Proc. International Workshop on Tenure Issues in Agroforestry. Nairobi, Kenya, ICRAF; and Madison, USA, Land Tenure Center. 412 pp.

Ramalho Filho, T.A., Pereira, E.G. & Beek,

K.J. 1978. Sistema de avaliação da aptidão agrícola das terras. Brasília, Brazil, MA-SUPLAN, BINAGRA.

Ridgway, R.B. & Jayasinghe, G. 1986. The Sri Lanka land information system. *Soil Survey and Land Evaluation,* 6: 20-25.

Roberts, N.A. 1977. *The government in land development: studies of public landownership policy in seven countries.* Lexington, USA, Lexington Press. 249 pp.

Romero, C. & Rehman, T. 1989. *Multiple criteria analysis for agricultural decisions.* Amsterdam, Elsevier.

Rossmiller, G.E. 1978. *Agricultural sector planning: a general system simulation approach.* East Lansing, USA, Michigan State University.

Schultink, G. 1987. The CRIES resource information system; computer-aided land resource evaluation for development. *Soil Survey and Land Evaluation,* 7: 47-62.

Thomas, P., Lo, F.K.C. & Hepburn, A.J. 1976. *The land capability classification of Sabah.* Land Resource Study 25. Surbiton, UK. Land Resources Development Centre, Overseas Development Administration.

Valenzuela, R. 1988. ILWIS Overview *ITC J.* 1988-1:4-14 (special ILWIS Issue). Enschede, the Netherlands, ITC.

van Diepen, C.A., Rappoldt, C., Wolf, J. & van Keulen, H. 1988. *CWFS crop growth simulation model WOFOST.* Documentation version 4.1. Wageningen, the Netherlands, Centre for World Food Studies.

van Keulen, H., Berkhout, J. A. A., van Diepen, C. A., van Heemst, H. D. J., Janssen, B. H., Rappoldt, C. & Wolf, J. 1987. Quantitative land evaluation for agro-ecological characterization. *In* A. H. Bunting, ed. *Agricultural environments: characterization, classification and mapping.* Wallingford, UK, CAB International.

Vargas, E. 1992. *Análisis y clasificación del uso y cobertura de la tierra con interpretación de imágenes.* Bogota, Colombia, IGAC. 113 pp.

WCED. 1987. *Our common future.* Oxford, UK, Oxford University Press. 400 pp.

Whitby, M.C. & Willis, K.G. 1978. *Rural resource development: an economic approach.* London, Methuen. 303 pp.

Wipenny, J.T. 1991. *Values for the environment: a guide to economic appraisal.* London, HMSO. 277 pp.

Wischmeier, W.H. & Smith, D.D. 1978. *Predicting rainfall erosion losses – a guide to conservation planning.* Agriculture Handbook 557. Washington, DC, USDA. 58 pp.

Wood, S.R. & Dent, F.J. 1983. *LECS. A land evaluation computer system methodology.* Bogor, Indonesia, Centre for Soil Research, Ministry of Agriculture/UNDP/FAO. 221pp.

Young, A. 1986. Land evaluation and diagnosis and design: towards a reconciliation of procedures. *Soil Survey and Land Evaluation,* 5: 61-76.

Young, A. 1987. Methods developed outside the International Agricultural Research Centres. *In* A. H. Bunting, ed. *Agricultural environments: characterization, classification and mapping,* p. 43-64. Wallingford, UK, CAB International.

Young, A. & Muraya, P. 1990. *SCUAF: Soil Changes Under Agroforestry. Computer program with user's handbook. Version* 2. Nairobi, Kenya, ICRAF. 124 pp. (including program on diskette)

Zimbabwe Federal Department of Conservation and Extension. 1989. *Land-use planning procedures.* Harare, Government Stationery Office.

WHERE TO PURCHASE FAO PUBLICATIONS LOCALLY
POINTS DE VENTE DES PUBLICATIONS DE LA FAO
PUNTOS DE VENTA DE PUBLICACIONES DE LA FAO

25/1/93

• **ANGOLA**
Empresa Nacional do Disco e de
Publicações, ENDIPU-U.E.E.
Rua Cirilo da Conceição Silva, No. 7
C.P. No. 1314-C
Luanda

• **ARGENTINA**
Librería Agropecuaria
Pasteur 743
1028 Capital Federal

• **AUSTRALIA**
Hunter Publications
P.O. Box 404
Abbotsford, Vic. 3067

• **AUSTRIA**
Gerold Buch & Co.
Weihburggasse 26
1010 Vienna

• **BAHRAIN**
United Schools International
P.O. Box 726
Manama

• **BANGLADESH**
Association of Development Agencies
in Bangladesh
House No. 1/3, Block F, Lalmatia
Dhaka 1207

• **BELGIQUE**
M.J. De Lannoy
202, avenue du Roi
1060 Bruxelles
CCP 000-0808993-13

• **BOLIVIA**
Los Amigos del Libro
Perú 3712, Casilla 450, Cochabamba
Mercado 1315, La Paz

• **BOTSWANA**
Botsalo Books (Pty) Ltd
P.O. Box 1532
Gaborone

• **BRAZIL**
Fundação Getúlio Vargas
Praia do Botafogo 190, C.P. 9052
Rio de Janeiro

CANADA (See North America)

• **CHILE**
Librería - Oficina Regional FAO
Avda. Santa María 6700
Casilla 10095, Santiago
Tel. 218 53 23
Fax 218 25 47

• **CHINA**
China National Publications Import &
Export Corporation
P.O. Box 88
100704 Beijing

• **COLOMBIA**
Banco Ganadero,
Revista Carta Ganadera
Carrera 9ª Nº 72-21, Piso 5
Bogotá D.E.
Tel. 217 0100

• **CONGO**
Office national des librairies populaires
B.P. 577
Brazzaville

• **COSTA RICA**
Librería, Imprenta y Litografía Lehmann
S.A.
Apartado 10011
San José

• **CUBA**
Ediciones Cubanas, Empresa de
Comercio Exterior de
Publicaciones
Obispo 461, Apartado 605
La Habana

• **CYPRUS**
MAM
P.O. Box 1722
Nicosia

• **CZECH REPUBLIC**
Artia
Ve Smeckach 30, P.O. Box 790
11127 Prague 1

• **DENMARK**
Munksgaard, Book and Subscription
Service
P.O. Box 2148
DK 1016 Copenhagen K.
Tel. 4533128570
Fax 4533129387

• **ECUADOR**
Libri Mundi, Librería Internacional
Juan León Mera 851,
Apartado Postal 3029
Quito

• **ESPAÑA**
Mundi Prensa Libros S.A.
Castelló 37
28001 Madrid
Tel. 431 3399
Fax 575 3998
Librería Agrícola
Fernando VI 2
28004 Madrid
Librería Internacional AEDOS
Consejo de Ciento 391
08009 Barcelona
Tel. 301 8615
Fax 317 0141
Llibreria de la Generalitat
de Catalunya
Rambla dels Estudis, 118
(Palau Moja)
08002 Barcelona
Tel. (93)   302 6462
Fax   302 1299

• **FINLAND**
Akateeminen Kirjakauppa
P.O. Box 218
SF-00381 Helsinki

• **FRANCE**
La Maison Rustique
Flammarion 4
26, rue Jacob
75006 Paris
Librairie de l'UNESCO
7, place de Fontenoy
75700 Paris
Editions A. Pedone
13, rue Soufflot
75005 Paris

• **GERMANY**
Alexander Horn Internationale
Buchhandlung
Kirchgasse 22, Postfach 3340
D-6200 Wiesbaden
Uno Verlag
Poppelsdorfer Allee 55
D-5300 Bonn 1
S. Toeche-Mittler GmbH
Versandbuchhandlung
Hindenburgstrasse 33
D-6100 Darmstadt

• **GREECE**
G.C. Eleftheroudakis S.A.
4 Nikis Street
10563 Athens
John Mihalopoulos & Son S.A.
75 Hermou Street, P.O. Box 10073
54110 Thessaloniki

• **GUYANA**
Guyana National Trading
Corporation Ltd
45-47 Water Street, P.O. Box 308
Georgetown

• **HAÏTI**
Librairie "A la Caravelle"
26, rue Bonne Foi, B.P. 111
Port-au-Prince

• **HONDURAS**
Escuela Agrícola Panamericana,
Librería RTAC
Zamorano, Apartado 93
Tegucigalpa
Oficina de la Escuela Agrícola
Panamericana en Tegucigalpa
Blvd. Morazán, Apts. Glapson - Apartado
93
Tegucigalpa

• **HONG KONG**
Swindon Book Co.
13-15 Lock Road
Kowloon

• **HUNGARY**
Kultura
P.O. Box 149
H-1389 Budapest 62

• **ICELAND**
Snaebjörn Jónsson and Co. h.f.
Hafnarstraeti 9, P.O. Box 1131
101 Reykjavik

• **INDIA**
Oxford Book and Stationery Co.
Scindia House, New Delhi 110 001;
17 Park Street, Calcutta 700 016
Oxford Subscription Agency, Institute
for Development Education
1 Anasuya Ave., Kilpauk
Madras 600 010

• **IRELAND**
Publications Section, Stationery Office
4-5 Harcourt Road
Dublin 2

• **ITALY**
FAO (See last column)
Libreria Scientifica Dott. Lucio de
Biasio "Aeiou"
Via Coronelli 6
20146 Milano
Libreria Concessionaria Sansoni S.p.A.
"Licosa"
Via Duca di Calabria 1/1
50125 Firenze
Libreria Internazionale Rizzoli
Galleria Colonna, Largo Chigi
00187 Roma

• **JAPAN**
Maruzen Company Ltd
P.O. Box 5050
Tokyo International 100-31

• **KENYA**
Text Book Centre Ltd
Kijabe Street, P.O. Box 47540
Nairobi

• **KOREA, REP. OF**
Eulyoo Publishing Co. Ltd
46-1 Susong-Dong, Jongro-Gu
P.O. Box 362, Kwangwha-Mun
Seoul 110

• **KUWAIT**
The Kuwait Bookshops Co. Ltd
P.O. Box 2942
Safat

• **LUXEMBOURG**
M.J. De Lannoy
202, avenue du Roi
1060 Bruxelles (Belgique)

- **MAROC**
Librairie "Aux Belles Images"
281, avenue Mohammed V
Rabat

- **MEXICO**
Librería, Universidad Autónoma de Chapingo
56230 Chapingo
Libros y Editoriales S.A.
Av. Progreso N° 202-1° Piso A
Apdo Postal 18922 Col. Escandón
11800 México D.F.
Only machine readable products:
Grupo Qualita
Kansas N° 38 Colonia Nápoles
03810 México D.F.
Tel. 682-3333

- **NETHERLANDS**
Roodveldt Import B.V.
Browersgracht 288
1013 HG Amsterdam
SDU Publishers Plantijnstraat
Christoffel Plantijnstraat 2
P.O. Box 20014
2500 EA The Hague

- **NEW ZEALAND**
Legislation Services
P.O. Box 12418
Thorndon, Wellington

- **NICARAGUA**
Librería Universitaria, Universidad Centroamericana
Apartado 69
Managua

- **NIGERIA**
University Bookshop (Nigeria) Ltd
University of Ibadan
Ibadan

- **NORTH AMERICA**
Publications:
UNIPUB
4611/F, Assembly Drive
Lanham MD 20706-4391, USA
Toll-free   800 233-0504 (Canada)
             800 274-4888 (USA)
Fax   301-459-0056
Periodicals:
Ebsco Subscription Services
P.O. Box 1431
Birmingham AL 35201-1431, USA
Tel. (205) 991-6600
Telex   78-2661
Fax (205) 991-1449
The Faxon Company Inc.
15 Southwest Park
Westwood MA 02090, USA
Tel. 6117-329-3350
Telex95-1980
Cable   F W Faxon Wood

- **NORWAY**
Narvesen Info Center
Bertrand Narvesens vei 2
P.O. Box 6125, Etterstad
0602 Oslo 6

- **PAKISTAN**
Mirza Book Agency
65 Shahrah-e-Quaid-e-Azam
P.O. Box 729, Lahore 3
Sasi Book Store
Zaibunnisa Street
Karachi

- **PARAGUAY**
Mayer's Internacional -
Publicaciones Técnicas
Gral. Diaz 629 c/15 de Agosto
Casilla de Correo Nº 1416
Asunción - Tel. 448 246

- **PERU**
Librería Distribuidora "Santa Rosa"
Jirón Apurimac 375, Casilla 4937
Lima 1

- **PHILIPPINES**
International Book Center (Phils)
Room 1703, Cityland 10
Condominium Cor. Ayala Avenue &
H.V. dela Costa Extension
Makati, M.M.

- **POLAND**
Ars Polona
Krakowskie Przedmiescie 7
00-950 Warsaw

- **PORTUGAL**
Livraria Portugal,
Dias e Andrade Ltda.
Rua do Carmo 70-74, Apartado 2681
1117 Lisboa Codex

- **ROMANIA**
Ilexim
Calea Grivitei No 64066
Bucharest

- **SAUDI ARABIA**
The Modern Commercial University Bookshop
P.O. Box 394
Riyadh

- **SINGAPORE**
Select Books Pte Ltd
03-15 Tanglin Shopping Centre
19 Tanglin Road
Singapore 1024

- **SLOVENIA**
Cankarjeva Zalozba
P.O. Box 201-IV
61001 Ljubljana

- **SOMALIA**
"Samater's"
P.O. Box 936
Mogadishu

- **SRI LANKA**
M.D. Gunasena & Co. Ltd
217 Olcott Mawatha, P.O. Box 246
Colombo 11

- **SUISSE**
Librairie Payot S.A.
107 Freiestrasse, 4000 Basel 10
6, rue Grenus, 1200 Genève
Case Postale 3212, 1002 Lausanne
Buchhandlung und Antiquariat
Heinimann & Co.
Kirchgasse 17
8001 Zurich
UN Bookshop
Palais des Nations
CH-1211 Genève 1
Van Diermen Editions Techniques
ADECO
Case Postale 465
CH-1211 Genève 19

- **SURINAME**
Vaco n.v. in Suriname
Domineestraat 26, P.O. Box 1841
Paramaribo

- **SWEDEN**
Books and documents:
C.E. Fritzes
P.O. Box 16356
103 27 Stockholm
Subscriptions:
Vennergren-Williams AB
P.O. Box 30004
104 25 Stockholm

- **THAILAND**
Suksapan Panit
Mansion 9, Rajdamnern Avenue
Bangkok

- **TOGO**
Librairie du Bon Pasteur
B.P. 1164
Lomé

- **TUNISIE**
Société tunisienne de diffusion
5, avenue de Carthage
Tunis

- **TURKEY**
Kultur Yayiniari is - Turk Ltd Sti.
Ataturk Bulvari No. 191, Kat. 21
Ankara
Bookshops in Istanbul and Izmir

- **UNITED KINGDOM**
HMSO Publications Centre
51 Nine Elms Lane
London SW8 5DR
Tel. (071) 873 9090 (orders)
      (071) 873 0011 (inquiries)
Fax   (071) 873 8463
HMSO Bookshops:
49 High Holborn, London WC1V 6HB
Tel. (071) 873 0011
258 Broad Street
Birmingham B1 2HE
Tel. (021) 643 3740
Southey House, 33 Wine Street
Bristol BS1 2BQ
Tel. (0272) 264306
9-21 Princess Street
Manchester M60 8AS
Tel. (061) 834 7201
80 Chichester Street
Belfast BT1 4JY
Tel. (0232) 238451
71 Lothian Road
Edinburgh EH3 9AZ
Tel. (031) 228 4181
Only machine readable products:
Microinfo Limited
P.O. Box 3, Omega Road, Alton,
Hampshire GU342PG
Tel. (0420) 86848
Fax   (0420) 89889

- **URUGUAY**
Librería Agropecuaria S.R.L.
Buenos Aires 335
Casilla 1755
Montevideo C.P. 11000

- **USA (See North America)**

- **VENEZUELA**
Tecni-Ciencia Libros S.A.
Torre Phelps-Mezzanina, Plaza Venezuela
Caracas
Tel. 782 8697-781 9945-781 9954
Tamanaco Libros Técnicos S.R.L.
Centro Comercial Ciudad Tamanaco, Nivel
C-2
Caracas
Tel. 261 3344-261 3335-959 0016
Tecni-Ciencia Libros, S.A.
Centro Comercial, Shopping Center
Av. Andrés Eloy, Urb. El Prebo
Valencia, Edo. Carabobo
Tel. 222 724
Fudeco, Librería
Avenida Libertador-Este, Ed. Fudeco,
Apartado 254
Barquisimeto C.P. 3002, Ed. Lara
Tel. (051) 538 022
Fax   (051) 544 394
Télex(051) 513 14 FUDEC VC

- **YUGOSLAVIA**
Jugoslovenska Knjiga, Trg.
Republike 5/8, P.O. Box 36
11001 Belgrade
Prosveta
Terazije 16/1
Belgrade

Other countries / Autres pays / Otros países
Distribution and Sales Section, FAO
Viale delle Terme di Caracalla
00100 Rome, Italy
Tel. (39-6) 57974608
Telex 625852 / 625853 / 610181 FAO I
Fax   (39-6) 57973152 / 5782610 / 5745090